D0897882

CHRISTMAS IN SCANDINAVIA

MELODY FAVISH

CHRISTMAS IN SCANDINAVIA

Recipes and Traditions from Norway, Sweden and Denmark

*Merry Christmas to Frances
in 1982,
from Mary, with love!*

TROLL PRESS • BELLAIRE, OHIO

Frontispiece, *Christmas in Norway* by Æ. W. From the top: Father fetches the Christmas tree from the forest. The *nisse*⁎ eats his porridge. A small cabin is nestled among the trees. Two children hold the star of Christmas. Below, someone has been "drinking in Christmas." The central picture, with its sophisticated and mannered people, probably originated in a German or Danish rendering, as the Christmas tree was little known, even in Christiania (Oslo), in 1866. A child looks through a window to see a Christmas tree. Below, a pious woman sits alone with her child. Compare her attire with that of the woman in the center. At the bottom, two men who are dressed like *nisser*⁎ attempt to lead the pig to slaughter, while the birds enjoy their Christmas feast of the *julenek.*⁎

ISBN 0-9609890-0-5

CONTENTS

Norwegian, Swedish and Danish are very similar, with only small variations in the written languages. All Scandinavian words in this book are keyed according to Norwegian*, Swedish°, and Danish◇. As most Norwegian and Danish words are identical, the use of Danish alone is limited primarily to special recipes. If some words are entirely different, all language forms are used throughout the text. Otherwise multiple language forms will be used only in the initial appearance in the text. All subsequent references will be in Norwegian.

INTRODUCTION

The celebration of Christmas in Scandinavia has changed so much in the last four or five generations. Many traditions which we consider old date back only to the turn of this century. Some customs which have lost their meaning have been discarded, while new ones have been absorbed from abroad and incorporated into the Scandinavian tradition. Today's *jul**, Christmas, is a compromise between old traditions and new cultural impulses, and much of the Christmas celebration has changed in the past 80–90 years. Scandinavians have always valued their old traditions, and when they saw some of them fading, they made certain that they would not be completely forgotten. Thus, many historical preservation societies in Norway and Sweden, and some in Denmark, began to record personal histories as far back as 70 years ago, and these give us a good idea of how Christmas was celebrated around a century ago.

Most Scandinavian Christmas traditions derive from rural areas. In the 1800's, about 75% of all Scandinavians were farmers, but that figure has now dwindled to around 5%. The farm was the most important social and family unit, and life for most people revolved around it. The identity of a family was synonymous with its farm, and if it moved to another farm, it changed its surname to that of the new farm. Many families, usually related, might live together on one farm, so the farm became a kind of social structure. Even today, in some areas of Norway and Sweden, many families in a tiny village will have the same surname, having descended from the one larger farm in the region.

Most farms in Scandinavia were rather small. The soil was often rocky, and the climate was so harsh in many places that it was nearly impossible to eke out a living. Many families barely managed to survive, especially if they did not own land. There was never much food to spare, and famine was always a very real threat.

Since the farm families' entire existence depended upon the rhythm of the seasons, one may wonder how families on small farms could take time out from the hard work of survival to enjoy the luxury of Christmas. Christmas, however, came at just the right time, for the

larders were full, the grain was threshed, and just as nature was going to sleep for the winter, the hard-working people could take a well-deserved rest after the busy harvest season. For approximately one month of the year, the people could concentrate on something other than the hard work of everyday living.

The celebration of *jul*☆, or *jól*, dates back to pre-Christian times. *Jól* was a sacrificial feast celebrated all over Europe to ensure a good

Pre-Christian Feast of Jul by A. Malmström–A *skål*☆ is dedicated to the gods, as small *nisse*☆-like figures look on. Note the straw on the floor.

harvest. The exact date it was held is uncertain, but the sagas indicate that great feasts were held at midsummer and midwinter, and the length of their celebration varied from place to place. *Jól* means "feasts," and according to King Haakon the Good, who reigned in the early 900's, *jól* began on midwinter night and lasted for three days. The Vikings did not have a calendar accurate enough to determine midwinter night, so the date varied from year to year.

Christmas Eve on the Ship Vega in the Polar Ice by W. Meyer. "Out on the sea he will drink in Christmas." Not only the Vikings celebrated Christmas on the high seas. Note that the tree is secured to the ceiling as well as to the floor.

The first written record of the celebration of *jul*☆ is a verse from a poem called *"Haraldskvede"*☆ written by Torbjørn Hornklove around the year 900:

"*Uti vill jól drekka*"
"*Ute på havet vil han drikke jul*"☆
"Out on the sea, he will drink in Christmas"

The "drinking in" of Christmas refers to beer, which has played a principal role in the celebration of *jul*☆ since before Christianity came to Scandinavia. The sagas tell of great sacrifices of beer to the gods. The *jul*☆ sacrifice was really a dedication of the contents of the drinking horn to the gods Odin, Frey, Njård and Tor. Each man raised the horn to toast the gods before he drank from it and then passed it to the next person. The Vikings felt that beer and the feelings it produced enabled them to communicate with the gods. It did not matter where one celebrated *jul*☆, either on land with the family, in a hall with other men, or out on the fjord in a longship. One drank in Christmas.

The solstice was a time for celebration in most early cultures. The

Romans celebrated the feast of the unconquered sun, a kind of birthday party for the sun. When the date for Christmas was established in the year 336, it coincided with the solstice on the Julian calendar. The solstice feast was given a new religious context, and in this way, early Christians could celebrate both holidays. As Christianity became more established, the day was dedicated to Jesus, whose Father made the sun.

When Christianity came to Scandinavia, the day chosen for the celebration of Christ's birth coincided with the midwinter sacrifice. It was very important for the people to feast at the traditional times, and it was much easier for them to accept Christianity if it conformed to already established customs. The old traditions were wrapped in a new package. In this manner, the feast of *jul** and Christmas were incorporated, and some of the pagan customs passed into Christianity unchanged. These include the luxury of the menu, the drinking of special beer brewed for the holiday, and the name. Other languages have adopted Christian names: Christmas means Christ's Mass; *Weihnacht* means holy night. But the Scandinavians have retained *jul**, even though the priests tried to change the name to *Kristmesse**. Even in England, yule was the more popular word for the holiday until the 10th century.

CHRISTMAS IN SCANDINAVIA

Advent

The Christian church year begins at Advent, and in earlier times this was a period of fasting and paying penance. In rural Scandinavia, Advent was a period of warmth and preparation for the holiday, a kind of introduction to Christmas. Most of the rigorous outdoor work was finished, and even though there was still a lot to do before the real celebration could begin, everyday life took on a mood of eager anticipation.

The first of the four Sundays of Advent was a special day in church. Everyone who could spare a coin or two gave alms to the poor. On that same day, it was customary to cut twigs of birch or other plant and place them in water, to force them to bloom for Christmas. Today Christmas flowers are popular throughout Scandinavia. The Christmas begonia, *juleglede*☆, "Christmas joy," was introduced around 1890 and was the first special holiday flower. As greenhouses became more adept at raising it, the poinsetta, *julestjerne*☆, or "Christmas star," took over as the most popular plant of the season.

The wreath, which we associate with Advent, played no role in its celebration until the end of the 19th century, when it came to Denmark

---

Christmas in Dalarna, Sweden, by Emil Rosenstand, 1890. The vignettes show many aspects of a traditional Christmas in central Sweden toward the end of the last century. From the top: A *tomte*° and his two cats enjoy a bowl of Christmas porridge, while birds flock to feed from the *julkärve*°. On the far left, the skiers use a single pole for balance. In the center, church-goers arrive by sleigh for early morning services. They throw their torches onto the ground to make a huge bonfire. The interior of the church can be seen in the circle. On the right, the starboys perform outside a farmhouse. The roses of Dalarna, which are featured in much of the folk painting, decorate the lower center, and on the bottom, people of all ages enjoy a merry dance not only around the Christmas tree, but also into the next room. Note on the wall alongside the door are two mangles or old-fashioned ironing boards, a popular gift from a husband-to-be to his fiancée.

from Germany. In this wreath are placed four candles, one for each of the Sundays in Advent. One is lit each week, until all four blaze on the Sunday before Christmas. Candleholders of brass, either on a round or oblong base, are used to celebrate Advent in Norway and Sweden, but these have become popular only since around 1930. Both the wreaths and the candlesticks often are decorated with red ribbons, though purple has become a popular Advent color in more recent years.

The Advent star, which probably originated in southern Germany, was introduced in Sweden around 1940 and spread to Denmark in the 1950's. It is not so widespread in Norway although stars are used in Christmas decoration in general, and the streets and stores usually are decorated by the beginning of Advent.

Most Scandinavian children get up early every morning in December before Christmas to open the window of the day on their Advent calendars. These, too, are a new tradition which came to Scandinavia from Germany around 1930. The first Swedish Advent calendar was introduced by the Scouts in 1932. Today many kinds are sold, some with the traditional pictures, others with the most modern cartoon characters. Some open to reveal pictures, others hold trinkets and candy.

Advent calendars are easy to make, and many Scandinavian magazines feature designs and patterns for making them. Some are embroidered and are adorned with 24 tiny rings from which to hang presents. Others are made with numbered pockets. Perhaps the simplest Advent calendar is made from 24 matchboxes attached to a piece of felt. The advent calendar also can take the shape of a candle marked with 24 lines to be burned for a short while on each evening of Advent. Whatever the style, the Advent calendar provides a visual countdown to the holiday for the youngest members of the household.

Grönkålsoppa°

Kale was one of the green vegetables which kept the longest, thus it became an integral part of the Christmas menu in Sweden and Denmark. A member of the cabbage family, its name is literally "green cabbage" in all the Scandinavian languages. It is a hardy vegetable which grows well in the cold regions of northern Europe and the U.S.

Serve kale soup during Advent to start the season with the taste of Christmas.

KALE SOUP

1 medium onion, chopped
1½ tsp. margarine
2 T. all-purpose flour
1 quart chicken stock or
  bouillon
1 lb. kale, blanched and
  chopped
½ tsp. ground fennel
Serves 6.

Saute onion in margarine in a soup pot until soft. Sprinkle with flour, mix and let cook for one minute. Add stock slowly, whisking constantly.
Bring to a boil, and allow to simmer a few minutes. Add kale and simmer for 5 minutes. Serve with chopped egg or sour cream.

Safranspastejer,°

Serve these mild cheese and saffron pastries lukewarm with consommé, kale or spinach soup. The saffron adds more color than taste, so it can be omitted. Shortening is not available in Scandinavia, but it makes a flakier crust than margarine.

SAFFRON TARTS

CRUST:
1⅔ cups all-purpose flour
¾ cup shortening
2 T. cold water

FILLING:
¼ cup grated parmesan
  cheese
1 cup finely grated swiss
  cheese
½ tsp. saffron, crushed
¾ cup heavy cream
2 eggs + one egg white
Makes 20 pastries.

Make pastry with flour, shortening and water. Form a ball and chill.
Roll out between sheets of plastic wrap. Cut and fit into muffin tins or paté forms. Preheat oven to 400°F.
Blend cheeses in a bowl, then add rest of ingredients. Stir saffron into cream before adding. Pour filling into pastry shells.
Bake 10–12 minutes. Let cool a few minutes before removing from forms.

Julekake☆

Julekake☆ is a round sweet bread rich with raisins and candied peel. It is delicious with a cup of coffee any time of year. Cut the loaf in half, then slice and serve with sweet butter. Stale *julekake*☆ is great toasted and makes excellent bread pudding.

NORWEGIAN CHRISTMAS CAKE

2 packages active dry yeast
½ cup warm water
1 cup milk, scalded
¼ cup butter
1 egg, beaten (reserve 1 T. egg for brushing on loaves)
½ cup sugar
1 tsp. salt
1 tsp. ground cardamon
¾ cup diced citron or mixed candied peel
¾ cup raisins
5 cups all-purpose flour
Makes 2 loaves.

Dissolve the yeast in the warm water. Mix scalded milk, butter and egg in a bowl. When lukewarm, add the yeast. Add sugar, salt, cardamon and 2 cups flour and beat well. Stir in fruit and the remaining flour, reserving some for kneading.

Turn out onto a lightly floured surface and knead until smooth and elastic, about 8–10 minutes. Shape into a ball and place in a greased bowl. Cover and let rise in a warm place until double, about 1 hour. Punch dough down and divide into two parts. Form 2 round loaves and place in greased 8″ cake pans or on cookie sheets. Or, make a large wreath for Advent. Cover and let rise until nearly double, about 45 minutes.

Preheat oven to 350°F. Brush loaves with beaten egg. Bake for 30–35 minutes.

Quick Julekake☆

This is a baking powder version of the popular Norwegian Christmas bread. It takes less than an hour from start to finish, so it is perfect for that 10 a.m. coffee break.

QUICK CHRISTMAS CAKE

½ cup soft butter
1 cup sugar

Preheat oven to 350°F.
Cream butter and sugar. Add eggs, one

3 eggs (reserve 1 T. for
   brushing on loaves)
3 cups all-purpose flour
3 tsp. baking powder
pinch salt
1½ tsp. ground cardamon
½ cup warm milk
½ cup water
¾ cup raisins
¾ cup mixed candied peel
   or citron
2 T. pearl sugar or crushed
   sugar cubes
Makes 2 loaves.

at a time, and mix well. Combine the dry
ingredients and add alternately with milk
and water to the butter mixture. Fold in
raisins and candied peel.

Form into two round or oblong loaves
and place on a greased cookie sheet or
in loaf pans. Brush tops with beaten egg.
Bake for 45–50 minutes. Cover with foil
if tops become too dark.

Svensk Glögg°

Serving Gløgg☆/Glögg° to friends and family during Advent is a long
standing tradition in Sweden. This hot mulled wine tastes delicious on
a cold winter evening.

SWEDISH MULLED WINE

⅔ cup raisins
1½ tsp. cardamon seeds
   (remove from pods)
5 cloves
1 bit fresh ginger (optional)
4 strips orange peel
2 pieces stick cinnamon
1 quart red wine
½ cup sugar
⅓ cup blanched almonds
Makes about 4 cups.

Soak ⅓ cup raisins and spices in 1 cup
wine overnight.

Strain spiced wine into a saucepan and
add rest of wine and sugar. Heat but do
not allow to boil. Serve with raisins and
almonds.

Candles

Candles have become one of the important elements in the celebration of Christmas in Scandinavia, but this is only since the invention of the electric light bulb. Earlier they were an absolute necessity, and the dipping of candles was a normal part of the preparation for Christmas.

The traditional day for making candles was Katarina or Kari's day, November 25. Usually the candles were made with the fat left from the slaughtering of the pig, but any fat would do. The best candles were made of mutton tallow. Stearine replaced tallow in the mid-1800's. The wicks were usually twisted or braided of linen or hemp, later of cotton, with up to eight threads depending upon the size of the candles to be made. Some were so large that they burned for the entire holiday. Since most people were poor, they made thin wicks, so that the candles would last as long as possible. The wicks were attached to wooden sticks and dipped in the melted fat. The first candles made were the whitest and best, so they were used for Christmas.

Church candles usually were made from beeswax. The activity of the bees represented the Christian work ethic, and beeswax was considered sexless and free from sin. The flame was a symbol of Jesus, the light of the world. But beeswax was rare in Scandinavia and so costly that even the churches were forced to use candles made from animal fat.

As with all other aspects of the Scandinavian Christmas, there was superstition connected with the making of candles. If the weather was good on Kari's day, the candles would be good. The person in charge of making the candles should be pleasant and happy—if she cried, the candles would run.

Two large candles, *julelys*☆/*julljus*○, were placed on the table on Christmas Eve, to represent the husband and wife of the house. They remained lit until the next morning. These candles were thought to be invested with the magic of the holiday, so on Christmas morning the stumps were collected and saved to be used as medication for both humans and animals throughout the rest of the year. It was considered unlucky if these candles went out too soon, for then misfortune or death would fall upon the family. Sometimes a log was placed under these candles to insure their burning all night, and this is the origin of the yule log.

Grenljus°, branch or family candles, are a part of the Christmas tradition in Sweden. Small candles representing family members grow from a central base, rather like a tree of life. Some of these candles were very large, as were the families of 100 years ago. Three-branched candles to represent the trinity, *treenighetsljus*°, also were used to decorate the Christmas table. Because these special candles are difficult to make and must be hand-dipped, three-armed candlesticks have replaced them in most homes. These are used on January 6 to celebrate the Feast of the Three Kings as well, and sometimes are called *helligtrekongersljus*°, the three holy kings' candles.

Real candles or "living lights," *levende lys*☆, as Scandinavians refer to them, help to recreate the atmosphere of a time long gone. Even many churches which use electric lights most of the year use real candles at Christmas. Some families still have candleholders for the Christmas tree, and for a few moments on Christmas Eve, the tree is lit with real candles as it was many years ago.

Beer

Beer has always been the drink of the people in northern Europe. Mead also was important until around 1500, when liquor replaced it. A feast without beer was unthinkable, and until the 16th century, the expression for celebrating Christmas was *"drikke jul*☆*."* The old *primstav*☆*/runstav*○, the calendar stick used all over Scandinavia, marked December 25 with a full drinking horn and January 6 with an empty, upside-down drinking horn. In this way the early Scandinavians expressed the significance of beer drinking in their celebration of Christmas. People drank beer most of the time, but Christmas beer was special, because it had a higher alcohol content.

Around the year 900, King Haakon the Good proclaimed that Norwegians should celebrate Christmas at the same time as other Christians. He made it mandatory for farmers to brew beer for the holiday, stating that the celebration should last as long as there was beer. Each farmer was obligated to make enough beer for all those working for him and stiff penalties awaited those who did not abide by this law. Until well into the last century, people in parts of Sweden placed an empty beer keg outside their house to mark the end of Christmas.

The *Gulating*☆ law (This was actually a body of laws established from the end of the 9th century through the 10th century.) stated that each farmer and his wife should drink beer on Christmas Eve, and that the beer should be blessed in remembrance of Christ and the Virgin Mary and dedicated to a good harvest and to peace. This Christmas blessing parallels the Viking *skål*☆ (The Scandinavian word for a toast, *skål*☆, means literally "bowl," so in giving a toast, they dedicated the bowl and its contents to the gods.) to Odin, Frey, Njård and Tor, and if the people desired, there was nothing to stop them from including the old gods as well. For centuries Scandinavian farmers had depended upon these gods to give them the protection they needed. Even though they began to pray to God, they did not give up the others completely. They first had to make certain that the

Christian God worked. Eventually, the toasts to the old gods disappeared, and after the Reformation, also the reference to the Virgin Mary. Even as late as the 19th century, the blessing of the Christmas beer was important all over Scandinavia. The head of the household dedicated a *skål** to God before passing the beer bowl or mug around the table. Each person answered the *skål** by drinking from it. Some of the beer bowls of the 18th and early 19th centuries were carved in the shapes of animals, the most usual being chickens or dragons. The finest examples of these are painted in reds, yellows and blues and are now collectors' items.

Two 18th century beer mugs in the shape of birds by Mick Bray after a photograph by Lis Hals Stuve. Private collection.

The drinking of beer was accepted by the early church in Scandinavia, and it is easy to see the similarity between the blessing of the beer and the drinking of the sacramental wine. During the Reformation this attitude changed, and from around 1600 onward, the clergy actively fought against the drinking of beer. At first they were afraid that beer drinking would turn the people back to their old gods. Even today there is a campaign against Christmas beer in Norway, this time because of its high alcohol content, and this thousand year old tradition may soon become a thing of the past.

Brewing could begin any time from 8–14 days before Christmas. Anna's day, December 9, is marked with a tankard on the *primstav** and was the traditional day to begin brewing Christmas beer in many places. She was sometimes called "*Anna med kanna**," Ann with the can." In other places, beer was made earlier and Anna's day was set aside for the first tasting. Then the barrels were closed until St. Thomas' day, December 21.

Only the best grain was good enough for the Christmas beer. The farmers felt that the darker the beer was, the better it tasted. In Denmark and southern Sweden farmers used rye, while in the rest of

Sweden and Norway they used barley. Sometimes oats were blended with the barley, but oats never were used alone, for they made too light a beer. Hops were added for flavor, as well as juniper berries (gin is made from juniper) and more exotic ingredients such as pepper and even tobacco. Sometimes liquor was added to make an even stronger drink. *Vørterøl*☆, a very strong dark beer sweetened with sugar syrup, also was made. This beer is unique to Scandinavia and is used in some of the delicious dark breads for which this part of Europe is famous. Today *vørterøl*☆ is only a shadow of its old self— it is now alcohol-free.

Good beer was absolutely essential to a successful Christmas, because it was the center of the secular celebration. Both the men and the women of the household worked together to make the Christmas beer, and certain precautions were taken to guarantee a good brew: Beer was never made at the time of the solstice. It was made during a waxing moon, so that it would last longer. No bad words were repeated near the vat, or the beer would be spoiled. And a branding iron was placed in the vat to protect the beer from being cursed by trolls.

Many Christmas meals are served with both beer and whisky, notably *lutefisk*☆ and *pinnekjøtt*☆. Until the potato came to Scandinavia, liquor was produced only on a very small scale, for there were better uses for the grain. The potato was cheap and it could grow just about anywhere, so it quickly became the staple raw material for liquor. Aquavit, the Scandinavian potato liquor, usually is flavored with caraway, which grows wild in many areas. It is smooth and very strong and tastes best icy cold. Today an aquavit bottle is often frozen in a block of ice before serving.

Christmas beer is still a tradition in Scandinavia (though an endangered one in Norway) and the breweries usually start their preparations well in advance of 14 days before Christmas. Barley and hops are purchased abroad, as few Scandinavian farms grow them any longer. These must be purchased up to 15 months before the Christmas when the beer is to be consumed, to give adequate time for shipping and for production of malt. After the malt is ready in August or September, it is combined with hops and the pure Scandinavian water to make into Christmas beer. This mixture spends the next 10–12 days in the yeasting department, where the temperature is carefully controlled. After the yeasting process, the unmatured beer is stored to age for around 3 months. It is tasted regularly and is filtered just before being bottled.

Around the turn of this century breweries in Denmark started making special labels for their Christmas beer, changing them every year. The old ones are now collectors' items.

Christmas beer is the oldest holiday tradition in Scandinavia, and everyone looks forward to its arrival in the stores. According to the breweries, Christmas beer has a limited lifespan, because it is made in a special way, so it is available only for the short time around the holiday. But maybe some of that old magic is in it, for as soon as the holiday is over, it turns flat.

Mumma°

Mumma° is a Swedish favorite at Christmas. You will have to look far and wide to find a more unusual taste combination.

MUMMA

½ ts ground cardamon   Sprinkle cardamon in the bottom of a
¼ cup madeira or port   pitcher.
   wine   Pour in madeira and stir.
2 bottles light beer   Add beers and ginger ale.
2 bottles dark beer   Serve immediately.
1 bottle ginger ale
Makes 10 glasses.

Lutefisk

Making *lutefisk*☆/*lutfisk*○/*ludefisk*◇ was an important preparation before Christmas. Until the middle of the 19th century, fish appeared in some form on nearly all Scandinavian tables, and *lutefisk*☆, dried fish soaked in lye, was the most popular.

People today can buy *lutefisk*☆ ready to heat and serve. But in the days of old, making *lutefisk*☆ was an art. Preparation of the Christmas *lutefisk*☆ traditionally began on Anna's day, December 9, the same day set aside for the first tasting of the Christmas beer. The lye was made by steeping birch ashes in water. The fish was cut into manageable pieces and soaked in cold running water, for six days, the water being changed each day. Then it was placed in a lye bath for 24 hours or more, depending upon the strength of the solution. The final step was to soak it in cold water for two or three more days, with two changes of water per day. After these procedures, the fish was ready to cook.

The best time for making *lutefisk*☆ is during the winter, when the water so vital to its preparation runs icy cold. Even though modern technology allows for year-round access to top quality *lutefisk*☆, it is still considered a seasonal dish.

Legend says that *lutefisk*☆ was "discovered" when someone carrying a bucket of lye stumbled over some dried fish and saw that the fish regained its original shape and color on contact with the lye. However this came about, it can be considered a lucky find, because salt was expensive and difficult to get inland, and it was much cheaper just to dry fish. Drying is the earliest known means of preserving fish. Dried fish keeps indefinitely and was a staple of the Scandinavian diet for hundreds of years.

Most dried fish comes from the Lofoten Islands off Norway's northern coast, where they are cleaned, split and tied to racks to dry in the salty breezes for one to two months. Dried cod makes the best *lutefisk*☆, because it has a fine texture and a mild taste. One pound of dried cod makes about 3–4 pounds of *lutefisk*⁕.

Norway exported dried fish to England as early as the 9th century, and in the Hanseatic period, dried fish was shipped from Bergen to Germany. Even today Norway exports dried fish to Spain and Portugal, where the national dish, bacalao, is most often prepared with Norwegian dried cod, and to Third World countries, where it is an important source of protein.

Lutefisk⁕

The traditional method of cooking *lutefisk*⁕, in a pot of water, is not so popular as it used to be, for many feel that it allows for too much shrinkage and dilution of flavor. Here are several methods of preparation. You can decide which one best suits the purpose. Allow 1 lb. *lutefisk*⁕ per person, as much is wasted or disintegrates during the cooking process. Do not cook *lutefisk*⁕ in aluminum, as it discolors.

LUTEFISK

Traditional method:
Place fish in a pot. Add salted water to cover (¼ cup salt per quart). Heat to boiling and then remove from heat. Skim off foam and let rest for 5–10 minutes, according to the size of the pieces.
Drain well and serve on a warm platter.

Dry method on top of stove:
Place fish skin side down in a large saucepan. Sprinkle with 1 tsp. salt per lb. fish.
Cover and cook on low heat without adding liquid for around 20 minutes.
Pour off any liquid that accumulates and serve on a warm platter.

Oven method:
Preheat oven to 450°F.
Place fish skin side down in an ovenproof dish with high sides. Sprinkle with 1 tsp. salt per lb. fish. Cover with foil and bake for 30–40 minutes, according to the thickness of the fish.
Pour off liquid and serve directly from the casserole.

St. Lucia's Day

St. Lucia's day falls on December 13 and is a time of feasting, especially in western Sweden, where it is sometimes called *lille julafton°*, little Christmas Eve. The present-day celebration of Lucia originated in Vänern during the last half of the 18th century. The girls of the household get up before dawn to serve coffee and special buns to the rest of the household. All are clothed in long white gowns tied with red sashes. Sometimes the young boys of the house accompany them and sing the special Lucia songs. The leader, who carries the tray of food, wears a crown of candles and is sometimes called a *brud°*, bride. The head of the household often rewards the girls with coins. The candled crown is thought to come from Germany, where pictures in old books show the Christ child clad in white with a wreath of candles on his head distributing gifts.

Until the late 1800's, Lucia was exclusively a west Swedish tradition with origins in the upper classes. Students carried the custom to the universities in Uppsala and Lund and voted for the Lucia of the year much as universities in the U.S. vote for a homecoming queen. By the turn of the century, Lucia had filtered to most of Sweden. In 1927 a Stockholm newspaper began to have yearly contests for the city's Lucia.

The tradition of Lucia is known in Norway from Setesdal to Hardanger, especially in the coastal regions. The custom was not accepted in Denmark until after World War II. While St. Lucia's day is an important family feast in Sweden, it never has been celebrated as such in Norway and Denmark. In those countries, Lucia is more an official figure who visits hospitals and centers for the elderly to brighten up the winter day with the traditional Lucia buns and coffee.

St. Lucia was a 3rd century martyr from Sicily. Several legends about her exist. Some sources say that Lucia refused to marry after taking a vow of virginity and had her eyes poked out. Others say that

St. Lucia's Day by Frits von Dardel. Lucia and her procession serve breakfast. Note the little Lucia on the right. This watercolor dates from 1851.

because her mother was miraculously cured of a disease, Lucia took a vow of virginity and distributed her dowry among the poor. Her non-Christian fiancé reported to the Romans that she was a Christian and she was ordered to be burned at the stake. When the flames did not harm her, she was killed with a sword. The red sash that the Lucia bride wears is the symbol of her martyrdom.

The name Lucia derives from the Latin word *lux*, meaning light, *lys*☆/*ljus*○. Etymologically, Lucia and Lucifer are related, and in many respects, Lucia is representative of both good and evil. The light of day and the dark of night are both part of her nature.

According to the Julian calendar, the night between December 12 and 13 was the longest of the year, the winter solstice. Earlier Scandinavians associated the solstice with mystical powers and superstitions. No work of a circular motion, such as spinning, grinding, winding yarn, even stirring a pot, was to be done at the time of the sun's

St. Lucia's Day, 1884 by Henning Thulstrup.

turning. Strange things were supposed to happen at midnight—running water turned to wine for an instant, and animals got the gift of speech long enough to complain that they thought the night would never end. Even after the calendar reform of 1753, *lussinatt*⁺, Lucia night, still retained some of its earlier reputation as the longest night of the year.

All major women's work was supposed to be finished by St. Lucia's day, and in some places *Lussi*⁺, as she was called, took on the appearance of a female demon or hag with horns and fangs who punished lazy housewives who did not get their work done on time. *Lussi*⁺ and her pack of trolls were always hovering over the farms between December 13 and Christmas looking down chimneys to see that the house was in order. It was dangerous to be out at night when *Lussi*⁺ and her band were out, as she could carry away naughty children and adults who did not perform their chores. She served a function on the old farms as a pressure to get work finished and a threat to children who did not mind their parents.

Traditional foods for St. Lucia's day are saffron buns and coffee. The shapes of these buns date far back, but originally they were not made with saffron. Their origins are uncertain and may even date to pre-Christian times, for the solstice was an important event long before Christianity came to Scandinavia. The most popular shapes are the wheel (sometimes used as a symbol for the solstice), the pig, and priest's hair. These buns are sometimes called *lussekatter*⁺, Lucia's cats, as the cat also is associated with Lucifer and is a central figure in many folk tales in Scandinavia.

Gløgg*/glögg°, a hot spiced wine, is often served on St. Lucia's day and on other occasions during the Christmas season. Beer used to be the drink most associated with the Christmas season, but toward the end of the last century coffee became popular. It was a more dignified alternative to beer, and the temperance societies, which were very active in Scandinavia at the time, adopted the custom of Lucia to encourage coffee-drinking.

Lussekatter*

St. Lucia buns, or "Lucy's cats," have not always been made with saffron. Now, their rich yellow color is their trademark. These buns can be made into a variety of traditional shapes, which are pictured below.

ST. LUCIA BUNS

½ tsp. saffron
2 T. boiling water
3½ to 4 cups all-purpose
    flour
1 package active dry yeast
1¼ cups milk
⅓ cup butter or margarine
⅓ cup sugar
½ tsp. salt
1 egg
Raisins
1 egg white, slightly beaten

Makes 48 single coil, 24 double coil buns.

Pulverize saffron and pour boiling water over it. Let steep.

In a large mixing bowl, combine 2 cups flour and yeast. Heat milk, butter, sugar and salt until warm. Pour over flour mixture and combine. Add egg and beat with electric mixer for 3 minutes at high speed. Stir in enough of the remaining flour to make a soft dough.

Knead until smooth and elastic, about 10 minutes. Place in a greased bowl, turning once to grease surface. Cover and let rise in a warm place until double, about 1½ hours.

Punch down and divide into quarters. Divide each quarter into 12 parts. Make coils of these and form into rolls. Some shapes take 2 coils. Decorate shapes with raisins. Cover and let rise again until almost double, about 40 minutes.

Preheat oven to 375°F. Brush with egg white and bake 12–15 minutes.

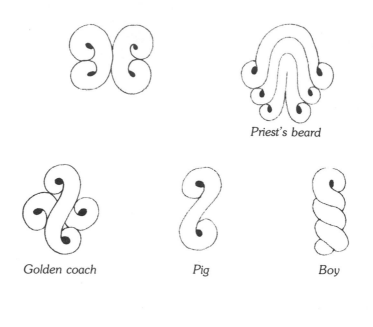

Priest's beard

Golden coach   Pig   Boy

Quick Saffron Cake

This variation on Lucia buns is made with baking powder.

QUICK SAFFRON CAKE

3 cups all-purpose flour
½ cup sugar
½ cup plus 2 T. margarine
5 tsp. baking powder
½ cup raisins
1 tsp. saffron
1¼ cups sour cream
⅔ cup water
1 egg
⅓ cup chopped almonds
1 T. pearl sugar or crushed sugar cubes

Preheat oven to 350°F.

Cut margarine into the flour and sugar with a pastry blender. Add baking powder and raisins.

Crush saffron threads and dissolve in water. Mix in sour cream and egg. Combine with flour and margarine mixture. Mix quickly to form a loose dough.

Pour into a greased and floured 9 × 13″ pan. Sprinkle with almonds and pearl sugar. Bake for 35–40 minutes.

Cool and serve directly from the pan.

Baking

One of the biggest and most tiring jobs before Christmas was baking. In much of Sweden and Norway bread was baked only two or three times a year, and it was not uncommon to bake batches with 150 lbs. of flour. Before anyone conjures up notions about the grim prospect of eating 100 day old bread, it is important to note that most of the bread was *flatbrød*☆, flatbread, or *tunnbröd*○, thinbread, thin crackers or wafers which could keep for many months. In fact, the 15th century historian, Olaus Magnus, wrote that flatbread ought to keep for 18–20 years. These crackers often were baked with a hole in the center so they could be suspended from the ceiling and taken down as needed. Some Swedish crispbreads, *knäckbröd*○, are still made with the traditional hole in the middle. The flour used depended upon the region and on the economy of the household. Barley and oats were the most common grains in Norway and central Sweden, while rye was grown in southern Sweden and Denmark. Wheat was a luxury, for it did not grow well in the harsh Scandinavian climate. Even the bread baked for special occasions was made of a rye blend.

Bread really was the staff of life in Scandinavia well into the 19th century. Part of a servant's salary was paid in bread, and gifts often were in the form of bread. To give bread was to give life. Bread was an important part of the celebration of *jól* even before Christianity came to Scandinavia.

One can see remnants of pre-Christian custom in the *såkaker*☆, sowing cakes, which were a feature of the Christmas table in Norway, Sweden and Denmark until the end of the last century. These round or oval breads were made with the last grain of the harvest and were richly decorated with figures pertaining to the harvest and with other, sometimes mystical, designs. They were left on the table for the entire Christmas holiday to absorb the special magic spirit of Christmas. The supernatural powers of Christmas could then be transferred by means of the bread. Crumbs were scattered over the fields to ensure good

The Christmas Table by Carl Wilhelmson. Note the pile of bread, the *julhög*°, on the table.

crops. Bits of the bread were fed to sick people or to nearly starved animals to give them magic healing and growing power.

Some of the mystique of bread is apparent in the Swedish *julhög*°, a pile of different kinds of bread which marked a person's place at the Christmas table until the end of the last century. This stack was highest for the head of the household, and diminished in size according to rank. Bread baked of the finest quality grain was on the top, and it was sometimes decorated with the person's name, or for the head of the household with a bird holding a kernel of grain in its beak, to symbolize hopes for a good harvest next fall. This bird was sometimes called *fredsduvan*°, the dove of peace. The stack of bread was to last until the Feast of the Epiphany, January 6, and in some places some was saved until Easter. It was the custom that one of each sort of bread baked in the house should be included in the *hög*°.

Lefse☆ was the main Christmas bread in Norway until only a few generations ago. The baking principles and technique were the same as for *flatbrød*☆—both are unleavened and baked on a *takke*☆, a kind of griddle—but lefse were usually made of better quality flour, rye or wheat, sometimes with the addition of potatoes. In contrast to flatbread, *lefse*☆ was always eaten while soft, spread with butter or sour cream, later topped with sugar. *Lefse*☆ is still a treat, though few housewives bake their own. Dry *lefse*☆ can be purchased in most Norwegian grocery stores. Dampened and spread with butter and sugar, it is delicious with a cup of coffee.

Hellekaker☆ or *lomper*☆ also were made for Christmas in Norway. These flat cakes were thicker than *lefse*☆ and were made of even finer flour with the addition of butter and later of sugar. Potatoes were sometimes used in these as well. *Lomper*☆ are served today in Norway rolled around hot dogs instead of buns. Waffles, made mostly of barley flour, were among the earliest festive cakes all over Scandinavia.

Æbleskiver◇ have been known in Denmark since the 1600's and were served on all festive occasions. *Æbleskiver*◇ means sliced apples, and the first ones were made of apples dipped in batter and then cooked in butter. Now they are usually made without apples and are served in many homes on *lille julaften*◇, little Christmas Eve, December 23, or on New Year's Eve. These puffed pancakes are also called *munker*◇, monks, although nobody knows why.

Flatbread was the norm throughout Sweden and Norway until well into the 19th century, when bakers' ovens became more widespread and yeast began to be manufactured. Even after oven-baked bread was generally accepted, it was still regarded as holiday food for quite a while. The tradition of yeast bread is older in Denmark, where people had easier access to yeast and to rye and wheat flour. In the isolated valleys of Norway and Sweden, yeast was unavailable except at beer-brewing time. At Christmas yeast was available, and some yeast bread usually was baked for the holiday.

Many of the cookies which we associate with the Scandinavian Christmas were unknown before the beginning of this century. It was not really until coffee became the drink of the people that cookies became popular. It was impossible to bake delicate cookies in the old ovens, where the heat could not be controlled accurately, though it was possible to bake cookies on an iron or a griddle. These are still popular today, and many Scandinavians couldn't imagine Christmas without *goro*☆/*go'rån*◇, *krumkaker*☆/*krumkakor*◇, or *strull*☆. Sometimes a woman with a *goro*☆ or *krumkake*☆ iron went from farm to farm to bake cookies. Cookie irons dating back to the Middle Ages have been found in Norway, and many families possess old irons with unique decorations, which varied according to the smiths who made them. Some had flowers and writing, others a lion or pictures of the Apostles.

Among the earliest known cookies in Scandinavia were *pepper-kaker*☆/*pepperkakor*○, gingerbread cookies, because they did not have to be fresh to taste good. Originally they were baked with pepper as the only spice. *peppernøtter*☆/*pebernødder*◇, peppernuts, also a kind of ginger cookie, came from Germany first to Denmark and later to the rest of Scandinavia. These Christmas cookies were made small and round to look like nuts and were made of rye flour with honey and strong spices.

Deep fat fried cookies have been known since the Middle Ages, but today's *fattigmann*☆/*klenäter*○/*klejner*◇ resemble the cookies of centuries ago only in the method of preparation, for the ingredients in these were beyond the scope of the imagination of that time.

Most early Christmas cakes were baked without eggs and with little sugar. Just why eggs were not used is something of a mystery. Perhaps they were so connected with Easter that there was a sort of taboo against using them at Christmas. Sugar was a luxury and was difficult for rural folk to obtain. Tastes changed as more people moved to the cities and could purchase sugar. Later raisins became a popular addition to Christmas cakes.

Today delicate buttery cookies are offered to guests throughout the Christmas holiday. Custom dictates that the hostess serve an uneven number of varieties, usually seven, and that does make a beautiful tray. It is not unusual, however, to bake 13 or 15 varieties.

Svensk Tunnbröd○

Swedish flatbread is usually made in large sheets, but small rounds are more practical for the home oven. Flatbread used to be eaten at every meal.

SWEDISH FLATBREAD

2 cups buttermilk
1¼ tsp. salt
½ cup sugar
½ cup melted butter
2 cups whole wheat or rye
    flour (or a blend of both)
3¼ cups all-purpose flour
1 scant tsp. baking soda
Makes 24 rounds.

Preheat oven to 425°F.
Mix all ingredients well. Divide dough into 24 sections and roll into paper-thin rounds on a floured board.
Place on cookie sheet. Prick all over with a fork. Bake for 5–6 minutes, until edges start to brown.

Lefse☆

Lefse☆ is one of the oldest festive breads known in Norway. This is a modern version, however, because it uses exclusively white flour. Spread with butter and sprinkle with cinnamon-sugar to serve.

LEFSE

5 cups mashed potatoes
  (can use instant)
½ cup light cream
1 tsp. salt
¼ cup melted butter
2¾ cups all-purpose flour
Makes 16 rounds.

Mix the first 4 ingredients together and let cool. Add flour, mixing thoroughly. Add additional flour if dough is too moist. Chill for 30 minutes.
Divide dough into 16 sections and roll each into a thin 8″ round.
Bake on a griddle until small brown spots appear on the surface. Turn and bake on the other side.
Cover with a towel after baking, so the lefser☆ do not dry out.

Æbleskiver◇

If you do not have the special pan for these Danish puffy pancakes, you can bake them in greased muffin tins. Even though the name means apple slices, there are no apples in this dish.

"APPLE SLICES"

1 cup all-purpose flour
½ tsp. salt
¼ cup sugar
¼ tsp. baking powder
¼ tsp. cardamon
2 eggs
1 cup buttermilk
½ tsp. baking soda
1 T. milk
Melted butter
Sugar
Makes around 20.

Combine dry ingredients. Add eggs and buttermilk and mix well. Allow to rest 15 minutes. Blend baking soda with milk and add to batter just before baking.
Brush each indentation of æbleskiver◇ pan with melted butter. Pour batter ⅔ full in each. Cook until golden, about 2 minutes, and turn with the help of a knitting needle. Brown on other side. Roll in sugar when done.
Note: If you are making them in muffin tins, fill cups ⅔ full and bake at 375°F. for around 20 minutes.

Goro☆/Go'rån○

Goro☆/Go'rån○ short for "good advice" are among the most festive of Christmas cookies. These rectangular cookies are made in a special iron, which is available in an electric model or the old-fashioned type, which is placed on a stove burner. These irons usually make 3 to 5 cookies at a time.

"GOOD ADVICE"

1 egg
6½ T. whipping cream
⅓ cup sugar
1 T. cognac
½ tsp. cardamon
1 cup soft butter
2⅓ cups all-purpose flour
Number of cookies depends on the size of your *goro*☆ iron.

Beat egg, cream and sugar light and fluffy. Add the cognac and cardamon. Mix in alternately butter and flour to make a dough. Sprinkle dough with flour and chill overnight.
Make a paper pattern of your *goro*☆ iron. Roll out dough and cut according to the pattern. Bake on a *goro*☆ iron until golden. Separate cookies while still warm, trimming edges if necessary. Store in an airtight tin.

Goro☆/Go'rån○

This recipe for *goro*☆ is perfect for using up the fat from frying *hjortetakk*☆ (Page 128.) or *fattigmann*☆ (Page 30.).

GORO

1 egg
⅓ cup sugar
½ cup whipping cream
Juice and rind of ½ lemon
½ tsp. cardamon
½ cup butter
½ cup leftover fat (lard or shortening) from frying cookies
2¾ cups all-purpose flour
½ cup plus 1 T. potato starch or ½ cup plus 2 T. cornstarch
Number of cookies depends on the size of your *goro*☆ iron.

Beat egg and sugar until thick and lemon-colored. Stiffly beat cream and add to egg mixture with lemon juice, rind and cardamon.
Sift together flour and potato starch (or cornstarch). Mix butter and fat well and add to egg mixture alternately with flours, beating until smooth. Chill overnight.
Make a paper pattern of your *goro*☆ iron. Roll out dough and cut cookies according to the pattern. Bake on a *goro*☆ iron until golden. Separate cookies while still warm, trimming edges if necessary. Store in an airtight tin.

Kringlor°

These Swedish cookies are a bit of trouble to make, but they are delicious. The lack of eggs and relatively small amount of sugar indicate that this is an old recipe. *Kringlor°* means pretzels, the traditional shape for the baker's sign.

PRETZELS

2¼ cups cold butter
3¾ cups all-purpose flour
⅔ cup sugar
4 T. cold water
Pearl sugar or crushed sugar cubes

Makes around 70 cookies.

Cut butter into flour and sugar with a pastry blender. Add water and mix as for pie crust. Chill dough for several hours or overnight.

Roll pencil thick lengths of around 6". Twist into pretzels or overlap ends to make wreaths. Dip in pearl sugar and place with sugar side up on a greased cookie sheet. Space well, as these cookies tend to spread while baking. Refrigerate for 15 minutes before baking.

Preheat oven to 475°F.

Bake 8–10 minutes. Cool cookies on a rack. Store in an airtight tin.

Fløtekjeks☆

These cream wafers are among Norway's oldest Christmas cookies. They are made without eggs and with very little sugar. These delicately textured cookies can be cut into your favorite shapes, but hearts are probably the most popular in the land of their origin.

CREAM WAFERS

1 cup sour cream
1⅔ cups flour
¾ cup butter
Sugar

Makes around 40 cookies.

Blend sour cream and flour. Cut in butter with pastry blender. Work dough to distribute butter evenly. Chill for 2 hours.

Preheat oven to 375°F.

Roll out dough to a thickness of ¼" Cut with cookie cutters into desired shapes and place on an ungreased cookie sheet. Sprinkle with sugar. Bake about 12 minutes. Store in an airtight tin.

Krumkaker☆

Krumkaker☆/*Krumkakor*○ are a favorite Christmas cookie all over Scandinavia. These cone-shaped cookies must be made on a special iron, which can be purchased in specialty shops and in larger department stores. *Krumkake*☆ irons come in electric models as well as the old-fashioned kind which is placed on top of the stove.

Old recipes for *krumkaker*☆ require the weighing of ingredients, and the best, most delicate ones do result from exact measurements. So, if you want to have the best *krumkaker*☆ in town, get out your scale.

KRUMKAKER

3 eggs
The weight of the eggs in sugar
The weight of the eggs in butter
The weight of the eggs in flour
1 T. water
Makes about 25 cookies.

Beat eggs and sugar until lemon-colored. Melt butter with water and add alternately with flour. Stir until smooth. Refrigerate batter for at least 1 hour.

Heat *krumkake*☆ iron and brush with a small amount of butter. Place a spoonful of batter on the iron and close, pressing hard, so that the pattern is imprinted on the cookie. The batter should just fill the iron, with no overflow. If the batter is too thick, add a little more water. Bake until golden.

Remove cookie from the iron and wrap immediately around a *krumkake*☆ cone (These usually are included with the iron.) or over a cup to make an edible bowl. Let the cookies harden and place them on a rack. *Krumkaker*☆ are delicious filled with whipped cream and berries for dessert. Store in an airtight tin.

Strull*

These cookies are baked in a *krumkake** iron, but they are rolled over the handle of a wooden spoon. They also can be formed over a cup to make edible bowls for berries and whipped cream.

STRULL

2 cups sour cream
½ cup plus 2 T. sugar
6 T. cold water
2 cups all-purpose flour
Makes around 40 cookies.

Whip sour cream stiff with sugar. The sour cream will become very watery before it stiffens. This should take about 5 minutes. Whisk in water. Sift flour over sour cream mixture and mix lightly. Bake as for *krumkaker**. Store in an airtight tin.

Strutar°

Do not despair if you don't have a *krumkake** iron. These cones are very similar to *krumkaker** but are made without special equipment. They are delicious filled with whipped cream and lingonberry preserves.

CONES

½ cup butter
⅔ cup confectioner's sugar
2 egg whites
¾ cup all-purpose flour
Makes 12–14 cones.

Preheat oven to 425°F.
Cream butter and confectioner's sugar. Stiffly beat egg whites and add to sugar-butter mixture. Carefully stir in flour. Draw circles around 8–9″ in diameter on parchment paper and place on a cookie sheet. You should be able to fit 2 per sheet. Spread batter into these circles. Bake for 5–7 minutes and form into cones while still warm. Store in an airtight tin.

Fattigmann☆

Fattigmann☆ are a challenge for even the most proficient baker. They are difficult to roll out because the dough is quite loose, and it should be handled as little as possible. It is important that these cookies be airy, tender and delicate. Too much flour will ruin them. *Fattigmann*☆ means "poor man" and today's interpretation is that these cookies are expensive to make, but years ago, the poor Norwegian farmer, who couldn't afford raisins and a lot of sugar, could make these with the eggs and cream he had on the farm.

"POOR MAN'S COOKIES"

6 egg yolks
6 T. sugar
6 T. heavy cream
2 T. cognac or vanilla
1 T. melted butter
1 tsp. cardamon
2 cups all-purpose flour
Oil or fat for frying
Confectioner's sugar
Makes around 80 cookies.

Beat egg yolks and sugar until light and lemon-colored. Add cream, cognac, butter and cardamon and blend. Quickly stir in flour. Do not use an electric mixer. Sprinkle with flour, cover and chill overnight.

Roll out dough as thinly as possible. Cut into diamonds. Make a slit down the center of each and pull one end through the slit. Heat fat to 350°F. Fry several cookies at a time until golden on both sides, around 2–3 minutes.

Drain on paper towels. Sprinkle with confectioner's sugar, if desired.

Klejner°/Klenäter°

The Danish and Swedish version of *fattigmann*☆ are flavored with lemon rind and are often cut into squares rather than diamonds.

FRIED COOKIES

1½ T. butter or margarine
3 T. sugar
3 egg yolks
3 T. half and half
1½ tsp. grated lemon rind
1½ T. cognac
1⅔ cups all-purpose flour
Oil or fat for frying
Confectioner's sugar

Makes around 45 cookies.

Cream butter and sugar. Add remaining ingredients in order, mixing well, Refrigerate overnight.
Roll out dough as thinly as possible and cut into rectangles about 3″ × 1½″. Make a slit down the center of each and pull one end through the slit.
Heat fat to 350°F. Fry several cookies at a time until golden on both sides, around 2–3 minutes.
Drain on paper towels. Sprinkle with confectioner's sugar before serving.

Pebernødder°

Peppernuts are among the oldest cookies known in Scandinavia. Centuries ago they were made with rye flour. They were brought to Denmark from Germany, and spread from there to the rest of Scandinavia. These small dark balls look like acorns, thus their name.

PEPPERNUTS

1 cup butter or margarine
1 cup sugar
1 T. light corn syrup or honey
2 tsp. baking soda
1 egg
1 tsp. ginger
1 tsp. cinnamon
1 tsp. cloves
3 cups all-purpose flour

Makes around 75 cookies.

Preheat oven to 350°F.
Cream butter, sugar and syrup. Add remaining ingredients and mix well.
Roll balls about 1½″ in diameter and place on a greased cookie sheet. Bake for 8–10 minutes.

Pepperkaker☆

Everyone loves gingerbread cookies. Most Scandinavians make hearts, pigs and goats as well as the traditional men and women. Generations ago, when spices were difficult to obtain, ground pepper was used to flavor these cookies, thus their name.

GINGERBREAD COOKIES

⅔ cup margarine or
　shortening
½ cup sugar
2 tsp. ginger
1 tsp. cinnamon
½ tsp. cloves
1 egg
¾ cup molasses
3 cups all-purpose flour
½ tsp. baking powder
1 tsp. baking soda
1 tsp. salt
Raisins for decoration, if
　desired

Makes about 50 cookies or about 35 gingerbread people.

Cream margarine, sugar, spices and the egg. Add molasses and blend thoroughly. Sift dry ingredients and add to the margarine mixture. Mix well and chill for at least 2 hours.

Preheat oven to 375°F. Roll out only a portion of the dough at a time, for it is easier to roll when chilled. Roll dough ⅛" thick on a floured board and make cookies with your favorite cutters. Decorate with raisins, if desired. Place on a greased cookie sheet. Bake for 8–10 minutes. Cool on a rack. Do not stack cookies as they will bend. Store in an airtight tin.

Slaughtering

Although most slaughtering already had been done earlier in the fall, there was still some left to do before Christmas preparations were complete. Since grain always was scarce, those animals kept over the winter were given very short rations. The pig was the one notable exception, since he was to be as fat and succulent as possible for Christmas.

In some areas the Christmas pig was slaughtered close to Christmas, while in others it was done as early as St. Lucia's day, December 13. In any event it was considered best to slaughter during a new moon, otherwise the pig would be difficult to bleed and the meat would be tough. There was also the risk that the meat would shrink, just like the moon, if the pig were slaughtered during a waning moon.

Every part of the animal was used. Hams were salted, trotters were laid in brine, sausages and head cheese were made. Even the blood was utilized in puddings and in pancakes. The fat that was left was made into candles and soap. In the self-sufficient household, nothing was wasted.

Pigs being fattened for Christmas

Sylte☆

Sylte☆/Sylta○ is time consuming, but for those who appreciate it, this traditional head cheese is worth the extra effort. Be sure to order the pig's head in advance. Veal is used in the sylte☆ to reduce the amount of fat and to hold it together better. Use proportionally more veal if the pork belly is very fatty. Make certain there is enough rind to cover the sylte☆.

HEAD CHEESE

½ pig's head
2½ lbs. lean belly of pork
   with rind
¾ lb. veal stew meat
   (shoulder is suitable)

SPICE BLEND:
1 tsp. salt
½ tsp. pepper
½ tsp. cloves
½ tsp. ginger
½ tsp. allspice
Whole cloves for
   decoration

Makes one head cheese, about 3½–4 lbs.

Remove ears and snout from pig's head. Wash well and soak for 24 hours, changing water frequently. Wash pork belly.

Place pig's head in boiling salted water (2 tsp. per quart) and simmer for about 1 hour, until rind is tender. Remove from water and peel off rind carefully, keeping it as whole as possible. Return pig's head to boiling water and cook until meat is tender.

Cook pork belly and veal in a separate pot, if the stock is to be used. Otherwise both can be cooked with the head. The pork belly and veal should take 45–60 minutes.

Have all ingredients for sylte☆ near at hand, for it must be made quickly, so the ingredients will not cool. Remove the meat from the pig's head and cut into thin, even slices along the muscle fibers. Cut the pork belly and veal in the same manner.

Dip a large piece of clean muslin into boiling water and wring out. (Cheesecloth is not strong enough unless doubled.) Lay cloth in a bowl and place outside surface of pork rind on it. Layer pork, fat and veal meat on the rind, sprinkling each layer with spice blend. If you have more than enough rind to cover the *sylte**, chop the rest and sprinkle it over the layers of meat. The gelatin in the rind helps to hold the *sylte** together. Cover with rest of rind and bind cloth around it. Sew cloth together and tie with string to anchor securely. The *sylte** should be about 5" thick.

Simmer in stock for about ½ hour until warm. Remove from stock and place under a press. (If you do not have a press, weigh it down with a dish and some heavy cans.) Do not press too much initially. Increase after about 30 minutes. Let remain under press for 24 hours.

Make a brine of 1 cup salt per quart water and soak *sylte** (still in its cloth cover) for around 8 days. The *sylte** ought to be kept in brine, even after it has been opened. Wrap in brine soaked cloth before storing in refrigerator.

Decorate with whole cloves before placing on the Christmas table. Serve cold with bread, pickled beets and mustard.

*Sylte**can be frozen for up to a month.

Leverpastej°

This Swedish liver paté can be frozen either raw or cooked. It looks like a cold meat loaf, as it keeps its shape. The anchovies lend a piquant taste. Top with sauteed mushrooms and crisp-fried bacon and you have the Danish version.

LIVER PATÉ

1 lb. pork liver
½ lb. pork belly
1 small onion
1 sour apple, peeled and cored
1 can (2 oz.) anchovy filets (Swedish anchovies are milder than those from Italy or Portugal, so you might want to rinse them before using)
1 T. anchovy brine (optional)
½ tsp. pepper
⅛ tsp. ginger
½ tsp. marjoram
3 eggs
⅓ cup all-purpose flour
1 cup half and half
Makes 12–16 slices.

Preheat oven to 400°F.

Clean and rinse liver. Cut into pieces and grind twice with pork belly, onion, apple and anchovies. Add remaining ingredients and mix well.

Pour into a greased 9 × 5 × 2¾" loaf pan. Cover with aluminum foil and bake in a pan filled with water to a depth of 1" for 1 hour. Check with a cake tester—if it comes out clear, the paté is cooked.

Blodpannekaker☆

The thrifty Scandinavian housewife made use of all parts of the pig, and that included the blood, which was made into sausage, puddings and pancakes. Scandinavians still are fond of iron-rich *blodmat*☆, blood food. Blood is available, frozen in liter blocks, and in Sweden, one can even buy a mix for blood pancakes. Blood is not allowed to be sold in many states in the U.S., but if you have access to it, you may want to try these pancakes. Blood binds, so no eggs are necessary in this recipe.

BLOOD PANCAKES

2 cups blood
⅓ cup buttermilk or sour milk
1½ tsp. baking soda
⅓ cup sugar
1 T. cinnamon
1 tsp. salt
Milk and all-purpose flour
Makes about 12 pancakes.

Dissolve soda in the buttermilk and add the rest of the ingredients. Add milk and flour to make a batter as desired—thin with little flour, thick with more flour. Grease griddle well and grease after each pancake, if necessary. Make large thin pancakes around 8″ diameter. Serve warm with butter and syrup or sugar and jam.

Värmlands Korv°

This sausage from the Swedish province of Värmland is made with raw potatoes. They can be frozen raw and then cooked directly from the freezer—they take about 30 minutes to cook.

VÄRMLAND SAUSAGE

6–7 yards sausage casing, about 2″ in diameter, cleaned and ready to stuff
2 lbs. boneless beef stew meat (chuck or arm)
2 lbs. boneless lean pork
4½ lbs. potatoes
2 large onions
3 T. salt
3 tsp. black pepper
1 tsp. allspice (optional)
1 tsp. ginger (optional)
Makes about 6½ lbs.

Grind beef and pork together. Peel potatoes and grind separately, discarding water that runs out, then grind onion. Blend all ingredients lightly but well. Stuff loosely and twist at 10″ intervals. Tie twice at each twist, so that sausage can be cut between ties. Prick with a skewer, cover with cold water and simmer, uncovered for 20 minutes.

Danish Pork Sausage

If your meat grinder has a sausage attachment, you will find this a very easy, tasty, and above all, lean sausage. Since it is low in fat, it can be frozen for up to 6 months.

DANISH PORK SAUSAGE

5 lbs. boneless pork shoulder
5 tsp. salt
1¼ tsp. white pepper
1¾ tsp. allspice
⅓ cup grated onion
2 cups stock left from boiling ham or sylte☆ or bouillon.
5½ yards sausage casing, around 2″ in diameter, cleaned and ready to stuff.

Makes about 5 lbs.

Cube meat and grind once on the coarsest blade. Blend in spices and onion. Gradually add liquid and mix well. Stuff loosely, twist and tie at 8″ intervals. Prick with a skewer and simmer for 10 minutes.

Cut into 2″ lengths and brown in oil or margarine.

St. Thomas' Day

All major men's work was supposed to be finished by St. Thomas' day, December 21. In earlier times, this was the first day of *julefred*☆, the peace of Christmas, and in Sweden was sometimes called *lille julafton*○, little Christmas Eve. (Today, most Scandinavians regard December 23 as *lille julaften*☆, and it is on this evening that the Christmas tree usually is decorated.) All threshing was to be done by this time, otherwise, it was thought, the rats would eat the seed, since legend had it that the resident *nisse*☆/*tomte*○ (See *nisse*☆/*tomte*○, page 86.) guarded the grain until that day, but no longer. Sometimes a small bit of threshing was left until Christmas Eve, in order to invest in that grain some of the supernatural power of the holiday. From this day until January 6, only a minimum of labor was allowed to be done, and those who continued to work were plagued with accidents. The only people who were permitted to work during that period were the clergy, and even their work load was lessened, for no marriages were permitted during the Christmas season.

St. Thomas' day also was the traditional marketing day, and before going to market it was custom to taste the Christmas beer. The beer was supposed to be ready on this date, thus giving St. Thomas the nickname Thomas the Brewer, *Tomas fylletunna*☆. This day also marked the end of the school year, and it was custom for schools to have parties. From St. Thomas' day, servants were allowed to sleep in the main house.

Jansons Frestelse○

The name of this dish comes from a story about a Swedish clergyman named Janson, who preached penance and denial, but was tempted by this delicious dish. "Janson's Temptation" is easy to prepare and can be featured as one of the hot dishes on the Christmas cold table, or any other time as an easy, inexpensive dinner.

"JANSON'S TEMPTATION"

5 *large potatoes*
2 *medium onions, chopped*
14–16 *anchovy filets, preferable Scandinavian (anchovies from Italy and Portugal are much stronger and saltier and must be rinsed before use)*
¾ *cup light cream*
2 *T. butter or margarine*
Serves 6.

Preheat oven to 425°F.

Peel potatoes and cut into thin french fries. Rinse in cold water and dry on paper towels.

Grease an ovenproof casserole and place half of the potatoes in it. Sprinkle with onion and distribute anchovies evenly over the potatoes. Top with remaining potatoes.

Pour half the cream and some anchovy brine (if anchovies are Scandinavian). Dot with butter. Bake for 20 minutes, then add remaining cream. Bake 30 minutes more, or until golden.

St. Thomas' day was the traditional marketing day before Christmas. Note the woman at the left selling a gingerbread goat and the little boy at the right buying a *kringle*✲ or pretzel. On this page, coming home with the Christmas tree, which was very small in 1865. The children are well-dressed with muffs and fancy hats.

Saffron Pancake

Scandinavians love pancakes, especially the soufflé-like ones made in the oven. This one, which is kind of a cross between a pancake and an omelet, is colored with saffron and is served with a sprinkle of confectioner's sugar and fruit preserves on the side. Serve for dessert after a light meal such as "Janson's Temptation."

SAFFRON PANCAKE

5 eggs
1¼ cups milk
1 T. flour
1 T. sugar
Pinch salt
½ tsp. saffron
3 T. butter or margarine

Serves 4.

Preheat oven to 375°F.
Dissolve saffron in a small amount of the milk. Beat eggs and add all ingredients except for the butter.
Heat an oven-proof skillet, preferably one of cast iron. Melt butter and let it foam. Pour in batter and bake in the oven for 15 minutes. Let the pancake cool slightly in the pan. Turn out onto a platter and serve warm.

Cleaning

Cleaning the house was an important part of the Christmas preparation. It was one of the last chores done before the holiday, usually taking place on December 23. In many places the house was cleaned thoroughly only twice a year, at Christmas and midsummer. Most houses of rural Scandinavia 100 years ago were really log cabins with one main room and perhaps a loft. These were swept out with a broom made of birch twigs. If there was a wooden floor, it was scoured with sand rubbed into the boards with bare feet. The fireplace was cleaned and whitewashed, and the chimney was given special attention, because omens for the next year would be read in its smoke. Since the housework was so arduous, some tasks were done by magic—it was tradition that the rats were told to move out of the house on St. Thomas' day.

After the house was cleaned, special Christmas tapestries or pictures were hung on the walls to make the drafty cabin warmer and cozier for the holidays. In parts of Sweden, these tapestries were paintings on cloth, mostly with religious motifs. In other areas, these were woven or embroidered. In central Norway they usually were woven in white thread with openwork borders and sometimes were hung over the windows like curtains. Poorer families hung up whatever they had, maybe a blanket or a shawl, to make their bare room festive for the holiday. In the north of Sweden these cloths remained hung for the duration of the winter, probably because of the need for insulation against the cold. No real decorating was done until the rise of the middle class. We like to think that the festive Christmas embroideries of today are a modern version of the tapestries of the past.

The barns and other out-buildings on the farms of old were dirty and dark. They were cleaned as well as possible with the limited means at hand, and crosses were drawn with red paint or tar over the stalls to protect the animals. Tar was preferred because it represented the growing power of the tree.

...iving area of a house at Donstad, Telemark, Norway by Söborg. This is the central living space ...f a home in southeastern Norway. The decorated clock, the iron stove on the left and the fairly ...arge window indicate that the family is fairly prosperous. The chair to the right of the room, known ...s a *kubbestol**, is carved from a tree trunk and is a common piece of rustic furniture.

All clothing and bedding had to be washed as well. This was a nearly impossible task in the cold Scandinavian winter. Clothes which were soaking often froze and had to be thawed by the fire. The only cleaning agents available were lye made from birch ashes, soda and sometimes a bit of soap made after the slaughtering of the pig. When the clothes were clean and dry they were pressed. This was usually done by rolling them tightly around a wooden dowel and then beating or pressing them with a wooden board with a handle at one end. This *mangletre**, which was decorated with carving or rosepainting, was a traditional engagement present, on which the groom-to-be showed his dexterity as a carver or artist. Now they are collectors items. Preparing the clothes was a tedious and time-consuming task. Until the late 19th century, most clothes were made of handspun and woven linen, a material which is difficult to press even with modern equipment. Clothes were then folded and stored in a large chest.

Most people wore their most tattered clothing in the weeks just before Christmas, so that the contrast with their new or clean clothes would appear even greater. Just before bathing they "killed" their clothes—they thrashed them so the bugs flew out of them. The Christmas bath on December 23 or 24 was for many the only real bath of the year. Usually the entire household bathed in a large tub or in the animals' drinking trough. In some places the animals were given the bath water to drink as protection against disease. Rank had its privileges, and father was first to bathe, then mother, the children and the servants. In Finland and in the areas of Norway and Sweden along the Finnish border, the sauna was adopted in the 17th century, so people in these regions were more used to bathing and did not regard it with the near panic of those in other parts of Scandinavia.

Julenek

The *julenek**/julkärve°/juleneg◇*, a sheaf of oats or barley for the birds, is one of the most popular Christmas symbols in Scandinavia today. *Julenek** are sold on every street corner and few homes are without them.

The *nek** has been featured in literature since the middle of the 18th century and first became popular in the cities and later spread to rural areas. What was probably adopted in all innocence by city dwellers who wanted to feed the birds during the cold winter months has become instilled with the spirit of the land, and the superstitions that accompany it probably originated on the farms.

The farmers thought that the spirit of the harvest resided in the last (or the first) sheaf of grain harvested. This was placed high above the house as an offering to the birds. It was very important for the birds to feed from the *nek**, and it was especially lucky if they flocked to it while it was being erected. If the birds ate well, they would not destroy the crops the following summer. If they did not eat from it, the harvest would be poor. In Norway, the *nek** was usually tied to a high pole, while in Sweden it was often hung with a cord from the eaves of the barn. In certain areas, it was thought to have special fertility powers. If a cow was unable to calve, she was fed grain from the *nek**. The same was true for cows who were due to calve before midsummer. During most of the calving time there would be little food. The magic power of the *nek** would compensate for the scarcity of ordinary grain.

The placement of the *nek** before sundown on *julaften** marked for many the true beginning of the peace of Christmas. After the *nek** was hung and after all of God's creatures had been given extra food, the celebration of Christmas could begin in the home. The *nek** also was a symbol of hospitality to guests. People who came through the portals of the house was offered food and drink, otherwise they were said to carry the spirit of Christmas out of the house. Miniature *neks** sometimes decorate the Christmas table in Sweden, and they are a popular subject for Christmas greeting cards throughout Scandinavia.

Placing the *julenek*☆ on Christmas Eve.

Surmelk Vaffler☆

These waffles are made with barley flour and are a bit heavier than those made exclusively with wheat flour. Barley flour can be purchased at most health food stores. Serve these waffles after a light meal.

SOUR MILK WAFFLES

2 cups sour milk or
  buttermilk
¾ cup barley flour
½ cup all-purpose flour
1 tsp. salt
1 egg
2 T. sugar
Makes 8 waffles.

Mix all ingredients to make a smooth batter. Let rest for 30 minutes.
Make waffles. Serve with sour cream and sugar or jam, or with butter and brown goat cheese.

Mørlefse☆

This is an old recipe for a festive kind of lefse☆. They taste best the same day they are made.

TENDER LEFSE

1 cup sour cream (pref-
  erably soured heavy
  cream)
1 cup buttermilk or sour
  milk
¼ cup sugar
¼ cup light corn syrup
2 tsp. hornsalt (See Notes
  on Baking, page 137.)
¾ cup barley flour
1¼ cups all-purpose flour
Makes 8 lefser☆

Beat sour cream, buttermilk, sugar and syrup. Add barley flour, hornsalt and half of the all-purpose flour. Knead lightly, adding more flour as necessary to make a smooth, even dough. Knead as little as possible. Let rest at least one hour.
Preheat oven to 425°F.
Divide dough into 8 parts. Roll each to a round about 10″ in diameter and place on a greased cookie sheet. Prick with a fork over the whole surface.
Bake for 15 minutes, until golden and soft. Repeat until all are baked. Stack as they come out of the oven.
To serve, butter each lefse☆ and sprinkle with sugar. Stack once again. Cut into diamonds.

Julehalm

Today we associate the evergreen tree with Christmas, but long before the tree became popular, it was the hay, *julehalm*☆/*julhalm*○, which was strewn on the floor which represented the spirit of Christmas. In Sweden it was sometimes called *julglädjen*○, the joy of Christmas.

Halm☆ has been used for centuries all over Europe, and in Scandinavia the custom dates back to the Middle Ages. Clean straw was strewn thickly on the earthen floor, making the dark, damp dwelling a dryer, warmer place for Christmas Eve. It was even strewn on some church floors.

On Christmas Eve all members of the household spent the night on the straw-covered floors and gave their beds to the spirits of dead relatives who were believed to return for that one night. The straw symbolized the first Christmas—all people could sleep in the straw as in a manger for one night. The dreams experienced by those sleeping in the straw were regarded as important omens. In some areas the straw was carried out on the second day of Christmas, December 26, while in others it was not removed until St. Knud's day in January.

Halm☆ became less popular in the middle of the 19th century, as wooden floors replaced earthen ones. It was a tremendous fire hazard and eventually was forbidden by law.

Christmastime by O. W. This picture is probably Danish, although it appeared in a Norwegian magazine. The landscape, with its babbling brook and leafy trees is more reminiscent of Denmark or even northern Germany than Norway or Sweden. At the top: Mittens and skateblades, a man ice-fishing and a boy on a sled. In the center, a family encircles the Christmas tree. The Christmas tree was almost unknown north of Denmark at this time, 1867. The family wear the clothes of the urban upper class, who were the first to adopt the tree as part of the home celebration of Christmas. Below, a child looks out at the julenek☆ and a nisse looks at his meal of porridge. Attached to the small fir tree is a mask, probably for the julebukk.☆

Tor's Feast by Per Hörberg. The caption on this picture from 1812 is as follows: "Tor's Feast, which was celebrated at the winter solstice and was called *jul*°: which is still called that in Sweden and is celebrated in much the same manner." People

are dancing, drinking beer, eating a pig's head, playing games and toasting the king in this *julstuga*° of long ago. Note the runic inscriptions on the back wall and the straw on the floor.

Most of the activities of *julaften*✲/*julafton*○ took place in the halm. The simple cabins of rural Scandinavia had few pieces of furniture, and with the gathering of the extended family, most people had to sit on the floor as well as sleep on it. It was only natural that the children and adults both should invent games to play and make decorative figures out of the straw. The making of straw figures had long been part of the pagan harvest festival of *jól,* and this was transferred to the Christian celebration as well. The spirit of the grain was believed to reside in the last (in some places, the first) sheaf harvested. The spirit could take any shape, but most often it was a goat. Even today, goats made out of one sheaf of grain decorate many Scandinavian homes at Christmas. This custom probably originated in Sweden, but it is widespread throughout Scandinavia. Sometimes the last sheaf was used to make a *nek*✲ to feed the birds.

Mobiles of straw diamonds decorated with red ribbons often were hung over the Christmas table. Their movement was thought to scare away the witches who were especially active during Christmas. Crosses and birds symbolizing peace and the holy spirit also were hung from the ceiling.

Today *halm*✲ ornaments decorate most Scandinavian Christmas trees, and making these birds, angels, and stars is an evening pastime for many families in the weeks preceding Christmas. These tiny ornaments are all that remain of this old custom.

Christmas Eve

On *julaften*✧/*julafton*○, Christmas Eve, preparation reached a peak. The men of the farm went out before dawn to chop wood. They usually only chopped enough wood for one day, but on *julaften*✧ they chopped enough to last for many days. The women of the house did the last of the cleaning and put away all tools of labor. The *halm*✧ was brought in for strewing on the floor, and the Christmas wall hanging was hung in its honored place. In some areas, people bathed on *julaften*✧, but usually this was done the previous evening.

Two dinners often were served on *julaften*✧, so that the people who were used to retiring early would be encouraged to remain awake for the *skål*✧ at midnight marking the birth of Christ. Some people stayed up all night, while others slept in the straw between meals. This was the Scandinavian version of the vigil, a remnant of the Catholic period. The *julestuer*✧/*julgillar*○ "Christmas rooms," probably originated in these night watches. With time, the tone became less religious and eventually these developed into regular parties. Since church law required the peace of Christmas to be observed, *julestuer*✧ were postponed until after Christmas Day. More religious families prayed in the straw, while most just enjoyed the company of the family and made small figures or played simple games.

It was the custom in many areas to set a place at the table for any relatives who had died since the previous Christmas, or to set for one more guest than was expected, so that nobody should feel unwelcome.

It was not the tradition to have guests on *julaften*✧, but no traveller was denied a place to stay. Even outlaws could seek shelter on the farms on Christmas Eve and Christmas Day, for a kind of temporary amnesty was in effect. Some farms took in paying guests over the holiday. These usually were bachelors who lived far away from their families. They were called *julegriser*✧, Christmas pigs, and they paid for their stay either with money or with work at harvest time.

The spirits of dead relatives were believed to revisit their homes on

Christmas Eve. Many people slept in the straw and gave their beds to their deceased relatives. Food was left on the dinner table all night for them as well.

For the superstitious rural people of Scandinavia, Christmas Eve was considered the most dangerous night of the year—this is part of the magic power associated with the holiday, which is a remnant from earlier times. Nature made it dangerous to be out during the dark nights, with the howling winds and weather and only the moon for light. These simple folk had a vivid sense of the nearness of the supernatural, and they could imagine all sorts of trolls and witches behind the strange noises. Nobody ventured outside for fear of meeting bands of witches and other supernatural beings. They were afraid of the *Åsgårdsrei*☆, bands of spirits on horseback who could carry off people. This vivid sense of the dangerous unknown and the imagination of the people made *julaften*☆ a favorite time for telling ghost stories. The ghosts represented all of the aspects of nature and of life that could not be explained.

These 7 cookie recipes make a lovely platter for Christmas Eve. It is tradition to serve an odd number. All of these cookies date from around the turn of this century:

Sandkaker☆/Mandelmusslor◇/Sandkager◇

Sandkaker☆ are a Christmas favorite throughout Scandinavia. These are made with nuts, but without egg.

SANDKAKER

1 cup soft butter
2 cups confectioner's sugar
2 cups all-purpose flour
½ cup finely ground almonds

Makes about 40 cookies.

Cream butter and confectioner's sugar light and fluffy. Add flour and nuts, and mix thoroughly. Chill for at least 1 hour. Preheat oven to 350°F.

Press dough into greased *sandkake*☆ forms with a floured finger. Place forms on a cookie sheet. Bake for 12 minutes, or until just golden. Cool slightly before removing from forms. Store in an airtight tin.

Christmas Work and Christmas Play by Johan August Malmström. Children Dance around the Christmas tree to the tune of a fiddler. The small vignettes around the central picture all feature aspects of the Christmas celebration. Counterclockwise from the top left: The *julhög*°, a pile of different breads, decorated with gingerbread goat, man and pig; fetching Christmas trees; baking rings of crispbread, which are hung behind the woman on the left; beating an animal skin rug; making beer; butchering the pig; the *tomte*° with his porridge; dancing and having a merry time; a happy *nisse*☆, as a mouse looks over the rim of the empty bowl; the visit of the starboys; drinking a *skål*☆ to the Christmas meal; in church; going to church by torchlight; the *julebukk*☆ distributing presents; the presents; people of all ages dancing around the Christmas tree; serving the Christmas dinner—note the three-armed candlestick; decorating the Christmas tree.

Berlinerkranser*

Berlin wreaths are one of the best loved Norwegian Christmas cookies. No platter of cookies should be without them.

BERLIN WREATHS

2 hard-boiled egg yolks
2 raw egg yolks
½ cup sugar
1 cup unsalted butter
3 cups all-purpose flour

DECORATION:
Beaten egg white
Pearl sugar or crushed sugar cubes

Makes around 70 cookies.

Mash cooked egg yolks, and blend with raw yolks. Add sugar and beat until thick and lemon-colored. Work in butter and flour. Refrigerate for at least 30 minutes. Roll dough into pencil-thick rolls about 5" long. Cross ends to form a wreath. If the dough becomes too soft, refrigerate for a while.

Dip wreaths first in egg white and then in pearl sugar. Place on a greased cookie sheet. Refrigerate 10 minutes. Preheat oven to 375°F. Bake 7–10 minutes, or until just golden. Store in an airtight tin.

Pleskener*

*Pleskener** are drop cookies which came to Scandinavia from Germany. They are simple to make, but remember to have potato starch or cornstarch on hand.

PLESKENER

2 eggs
2 egg yolks
1¼ cups sugar
1½ cups all-purpose flour
⅔ cup potato starch or
¾ cup cornstarch
2 tsp. baking powder
Candied peel
Makes 60 cookies.

Preheat oven to 350°F.
Beat eggs, egg yolks and sugar until thick and lemon-colored. Add flour, starch and baking powder.
Form cookies with a spoon and place on ungreased cookie sheet. Place a small piece of candied peel on each cookie. Bake 6–8 minutes. Store in an airtight tin.

Bordstabelbakkels*

*Bordstabel** means a pile of lumber, and these cookies are stacked two by two, forming a square pile, for serving. These long, thin cookies are very delicate.

"LOG PILES"

1 egg
1 T. light cream
½ cup sugar
2 cups all-purpose flour
1 cup soft unsalted butter
1 batch marzipan (See page 00)
½ egg white
Makes around 80 cookies.

Beat egg, cream and sugar until light and fluffy. Mix in flour and soft butter. Knead lightly a few times to distribute butter throughout dough. Chill for at least 1 hour.

Make marzipan. Thin with ½ egg white for easier spreading

Preheat oven to 350°F.

Roll out dough about ¼" thick. Cut out 4" by 1" strips with a pastry wheel, and place on a greased cookie sheet. Spoon marzipan in thin strips on top of cookies. Bake for 6–8 minutes, or until marzipan just begins to turn golden.

Serinakaker*

*Serinakaker** can be recognized by the marks of the fork tines used for flattening them. Nobody knows how serina cakes got their name.

SERINA CAKES

1⅔ cups all-purpose flour
½ cup sugar
¼ tsp. hornsalt (See Notes on Baking, page 137.)
⅔ cup butter or margarine
1 egg
½ tsp. vanilla
Beaten egg white
Chopped almonds
Pearl sugar
Makes about 90 cookies.

Preheat oven to 350°F. Mix dry ingredients. Cut in butter with a pastry blender. Add egg and vanilla and mix quickly to form a dough.

Make small balls and place on a greased cookie sheet. Press flat with the tines of a fork. Brush with beaten egg white and sprinkle with chopped almonds and pearl sugar.

Bake 10–12 minutes. Store in an airtight tin.

Mor Monsen*

The name is catchy, but nobody knows who Mother Monsen was. This is really a cake, but it is considered one of the traditional Norwegian Christmas "cookies." Cut small, diamond-shaped pieces to serve.

MOTHER MONSEN

1 cup butter or margarine
1 cup sugar
4 eggs
1⅔ cups all-purpose flour
1 tsp. baking powder
2 tsp. lemon juice
1 tsp. vanilla
3–4 T. chopped almonds
¼ cup currants or raisins
3–4 T. pearl sugar or crushed sugar cubes

Preheat oven to 375°F.
Cream butter and sugar until light and fluffy. Blend in egg yolks, flour, baking powder, lemon juice and vanilla. Beat egg whites until stiff and fold into batter.
Pour into a greased and floured 9″ square cake pan. Sprinkle with nuts, currants and sugar. Bake for 30 minutes.

Spice Macaroons

These almond macaroons are flavored with cloves and cardamon.

SPICE MACAROONS

4 egg whites
½ tsp. ground cloves
1½ tsp. ground cardamon
¾ cup sugar
2 cups slivered almonds
Makes around 50 cookies.

Preheat oven to 375°F.
Beat egg whites until stiff. Stir spices into sugar and carefully fold into egg whites. Fold in nuts.
Place spoonfuls of batter on a greased cookie sheet. Bake for about 35 minutes, until light and crispy.

Religion

Although Christmas always has been the most important holiday of the year for Scandinavians, the emphasis is more on the family and the home than on the church. Religion was a natural part of everyday life, and the hard working Scandinavian farmers were the embodiment of the Protestant work ethic. All of the preparations before Christmas had a reverent aspect and were thought to be just as important as attending church.

Until the early years of this century, religious services often were conducted in the home on Christmas Eve, with the children singing prayers before the first dinner and father reading the story of Christmas afterwards. Often the only books found in the home were Bibles, prayerbooks and hymnals, for few could read. Even with the beginning of the public schools in the 1840's, literacy was slow in coming to the more remote farms, for most children had to work in the fields, and school attendance was sporadic.

Toward the middle of the 19th century, many areas were influenced by the Free Church movements, and religious services played a much greater role in the celebration of Christmas in these dissenting societies, which were predominant in certain areas of Norway and Sweden.

Today many families in Sweden, Norway and Denmark attend Vespers on Christmas Eve. These services begin just after the ringing in of Christmas at 5 p.m. Many remember their departed loved ones at this time by placing candles and wreaths of reindeer moss by the graves. Although it is an old custom to honor the dead by lighting candles on special days of the year, the placing of candles and wreaths on the graves is a relatively new practice, dating in Norway from around 1920 and believed to have originated in Sweden. This custom was transferred from All Saints' day, November 1, which is still a public holiday there.

Dansk Gløgg◇

Danish *gløgg*◇ is a bit sweeter than its Swedish counterpart. It tastes best when made the night before serving so that the flavors can blend well.

DANISH MULLED WINE

1 cup boiling water
1¼ cups sugar
5 large pieces stick cinnamon
20 cloves
2 tsp. whole cardamon
2 strips orange peel
2 small bits fresh ginger (optional)
¾ cup rum
¾ cup raisins
¾ cup blanched almonds
2 bottles (6 cups) red wine
Makes approximately 2 quarts.

Dissolve sugar in boiling water. Add spices and boil for 10 minutes. Add rum and raisins and let steep overnight or for at least five hours.

Remove cinnamon sticks, orange peel and ginger. Add almonds and wine. Heat, but do not allow to boil.

When serving, be sure to include raisins and almonds in each glass.

Grytten Kirke, Veblungsnes, Norway, by Mick Bray after a photograph by H. Sødahl

Food

Food is a major part of the Christmas celebration and was even more important on the farms, where the daily diet was monotonous at best. In many places the already meager food rations were cut on St. Clemens' day, November 23, especially for children, so that they would appreciate even more the bounty of Christmas. Today just the opposite is true, for one of the most popular kinds of party during the month of December is the *julebord**, a table laden with all the traditional Christmas foods. Many businesses and offices sponsor a *julebord** as a Christmas party for their employees. Restaurants begin publicizing their Christmas tables in November.

Every little settlement in Scandinavia has its own special Christmas traditions and foods. The foods people eat at Christmas depend both upon the region where they live and what they remember from childhood. With today's mobile population, the traditions which once were limited to certain areas now appear nationwide.

The eating of special food for Christmas traditionally started on December 23, *lille julaften**, in Denmark. On that day it was customary to eat pea soup made with the broth from cooking ham or *sylte**, head cheese, with *æbleskiver*◇ for dessert. *Saltmadsfad*◇, salt meat served in its own broth, with bread for dipping, also was popular on that day and sometimes was eaten early on Christmas Eve. Norway and Sweden do not really have special dishes for *lille julaften**.

It was customary all over Scandinavia that breakfast on *julaften** should be extra good and fat, but not as rich as Christmas dinner. In Norway the usual breakfast was *mølje**, warm fat thinned with some broth, served with crumbled flatbread. Sometimes it was topped with syrup or brown goat cheese. This was accompanied by beer and whisky, even for children. *Mølje** could be made of any kind of fat, and of course, the fat from the Christmas pig was considered the most delectable. But, along the coast, it was not unusual for *mølje** to be made of fish liver. It is hard for us today to understand just how a bowl of fat (especially fish fat) could be appealing, but Scandinavians a century ago had a meager diet of mostly grain, dairy products, potatoes and other root vegetables, augmented with a little dried fish or meat. Most people did heavy manual labor in all kinds of weather and lived in cold, damp log cabins. Fat, any kind of fat, was a luxury to them and provided warmth as well as nourishment.

Dopp i grytan° was the usual lunch in Sweden. Every member of the family assembled in the kitchen to eat "Dip in the Pot." Pieces of dark, spicy bread were dipped into the rich, concentrated broth made from the cooking of the Christmas ham. Most children preferred this to *julafton*'s *lutfisk*° and porridge. *Dopp i grytan*° also was a means to skirt the fasting rules—the ham was not to be eaten until Christmas day, but one could get a little preview by dipping bread into its broth. Whatever its origin, *dopp i grytan*° became a practical tradition during a busy time. In this way the hardworking housewife had one less meal to make.

One can safely say that until the middle of the 19th century, fish, accompanied by flatbread, beer and whisky, was almost exclusively the main dish on Christmas Eve in Scandinavia. Fish has appeared on the Scandinavian Christmas table since the Catholic period, when everyone fasted before holy days. The custom of eating fish at Christmas survived the Reformation, even though fresh fish was nearly impossible to get in some inland areas. In places where two Christmas dinners were served, fish often was the main course of the first, for tradition dictated that the first meal of the holiday should be lighter than the last—this meal was actually the last of the fast.

The most popular Christmas fish dish all over Scandinavia is *lutefisk*☆, dried fish soaked in lye before cooking. It is a good example of a dish which for hundreds of years was considered everday food, but which now is a delicacy. In a survey conducted a few years ago by a leading Oslo newspaper, *lutefisk*☆ was the second favorite Christmas dinner in Norway, outranked only by *ribbe*☆, roasted pork ribs.

Side dishes vary according to the region. Olaus Magnus, an historian of the 16th century, mentions *lutefisk*☆ served with salted butter. In eastern Norway, where it is most popular, it is served with mashed green peas and *ribbefett*☆, fat from the pork ribs. Most fish markets in this area sell containers of *ribbefett*☆ at Christmas. In other areas it is served with melted butter or fried bacon. In Gudbrandsdal in central Norway, it is served with *lefse*☆. A creamy butter sauce is a favorite in Finland, where this dish is known as *lipeakala.* Swedes prefer it with strong homemade mustard, white sauce and mashed yellow peas.. Beer and aquavit are served with this dish throughout the Nordic countries.

Lutefisk☆ seldom appears on the Christmas table in areas which have access to fresh fish. Boiled cod, *kokt torsk*☆, is the third most popular Christmas dish in Norway, according to the survey mentioned above, and is most often served along the southern coast. Norwegians are purists. They like their cod unadorned, served with boiled potatoes, melted parsley butter, and unique to Norway, red wine. *Rakørret*☆, fermented trout, is enjoyed in the eastern regions, while boiled halibut, *kveite*☆, is a choice dish in northern Norway. *Ål*○, eel is popular in Denmark, while fresh water fish such as pike, *gädde*○, and perch, *åbbor*○, adorn the tables in the lake regions of Sweden. No Christmas breakfast table anywhere in Scandinavia is complete without herring in marinade or herring salad.

Although it never became so widespread as fish, porridge was often the first meal of Christmas. It too was a remnant from the Catholic period, when one ate white food before a holy day. Porridge made from barley, oats or rye cooked in water was a regular part of the daily diet, but Christmas porridge was made from finer meal or flour cooked in milk. *Risengrynsgrøt*☆/*risgrynsgröt*○, rice porridge flavored with sugar and cinnamon, became popular toward the end of the last century and gradually replaced the other types of porridge for the holiday table. Rice was imported to Scandinavia earlier, but until around 1890 was too expensive for most families. Rice porridge is still eaten today, and in some families a single almond is added, and whoever finds it

Fish and porridge are two of the most popular and historical Christmas dishes in Scandinavia.

in his or her bowl gets a small gift, usually a marzipan pig. Rice porridge is rarely served as the main course at Christmas dinner, although many enjoy it for lunch or as dessert. Cold rice porridge mixed with whipped cream and served with a fruit sauce made of sieved raspberries or strawberries is a favorite at Christmas.

Everyone associates pork dishes with the Scandinavian Christmas, and the pig is a central theme in the celebration of the holiday, appearing on greeting cards, as tree ornaments, and in marzipan. The serving of pork at Christmas is an old tradition and may even be a relic of the pre-Christian *jól*. Pork was served at Christmas in England as well until Elizabethan times, and the presentation of the boar's head was an important part of the medieval banquet. In some areas of Norway, however, it is only in the last 100 years or so that pork has been served for Christmas. Before that goat or lamb were the usual dishes, for the poor farmers could not afford to keep a pig.

Ribbe☆, pork ribs with the bacon and sometimes the chops attached, is the most popular Christmas dinner in Norway, where approximately 60% of the population serve it on Christmas Eve. In many homes it is served with *medisterpølser*☆, pork sausages, and *medisterkaker*☆, cakes of spiced ground pork. Side dishes include *surkål*☆, a warm, caraway-flavored variation of sauerkraut and *tyttebær*☆, lingonberries or tart wild cranberries made into a jam or compote, and boiled potatoes. Today no dinner is complete without potatoes, but in Norway and Sweden a century ago, they usually were excluded from the Christmas table. After all, the potato was one of the staple foods of Scandinavia and was eaten every other day of the year. Today they have regained their proper place.

Skinke○, a lightly salted, lightly smoked ham, topped with a mixture of mustard and breadcrumbs, adorns the Swedish Christmas table, but not until Christmas Day. A Christmas without ham to a Swede is like Thanksgiving without a turkey to an American. It is a must! With the exception of the topping, a Swedish Christmas ham tastes very much like an American baked ham, as the salting and smoking methods are similar. The ham is usually a large, whole one, as cold ham is an integral part of the Christmas *smörgåsbord*○. Today side dishes include a variety of salads, but in times past, the most important accompaniment was *långkål*○, whole kale, which was first boiled and then browned in fat. Sometimes it was served creamed as well. *Brunkål*○, white cabbage, which was chopped and then browned in fat, was another popular side dish. Bread was an important part of the Christmas meal in Sweden, moreso than in the other Scandinavian countries.

Other Swedish pork dishes at Christmas include brown beans and fried pork belly, blood pancakes, and pig's trotters—in some places it was considered great sport to eat these, for it was tradition to drink a shot of whisky for each bone. In most places, though, the trotters were saved for New Year's Eve.

Pork dishes are popular in Denmark year-round, and the Danish pig is world famous. It is a lean pig and resembles only slightly the fat hog which was so prized in the past. It is longer, too, because it has been bred with an extra set of ribs, which allow for two additional chops per animal. A pork loin roast stuffed with apples and prunes or a fresh ham are the traditional Christmas pork dinners. Kale was the usual side dish in Denmark as well, and has been cultivated there since the Middle Ages. It is a hardy variety of cabbage, which tastes best after its leaves have gotten a touch of frost. But in Denmark, the pig has serious competition at Christmas: The goose, which has been well established for the last 150 years. Like the Christmas tree, it first became accepted among the bourgeoisie. Geese have been raised on Danish farms since the Middle Ages, but at that time, they were part of the payment in kind which tenant farmers gave to the lord of the manor. Thus, it was in upper class circles that the geese first were consumed. The farmers raised them, but they did not eat them. Even toward the end of the last century, they usually sold them to city dwellers, and continued to eat pork at Christmas.

Goose has been a traditional Christmas food in Germany since the 14th century. It was transferred to Christmas from St. Martin's day, or *Mårtensdag*°, when the goose played an important role—a honking goose revealed Bishop Martin's hiding place, and for that reason, a goose is sacrificed on his feast day. Some Swedes still eat goose on that day, November 11, for ham is too well anchored in Swedish tradition for it to be replaced by a goose for Christmas.

In the last 30–40 years duck has become popular all over Denmark, both in the city and in the country. It tastes almost like goose and is easier to prepare for today's smaller families. Side dishes for both goose and duck are *rødkål*°, spiced red cabbage, and *brunede kartofler*°, boiled potatoes which have been glazed with butter and sugar.

A more localized holiday dish is *pinnekjøtt*☆, originally a tradition on the west coast of Norway, the fourth favorite Christmas Eve meal. Lamb ribs are dry salted for 36 hours and then hung to dry from

Merry Christmas in Denmark by F. N. Møller, 1882. This could be called the *nisses'*☆ Christmas. From the top: The Christmas bell tolls over the moonlit Danish countryside. The merry little *nisser*☆ are having a holiday feast for their king. A *nisse*☆ and his cat sample the porridge and beer. A pair of *nisser*☆ dance (Note the appearance of a female *nisse*☆). A *nisse*☆ is preparing to carve the Christmas goose.

butchering time in September or October until Christmas, a minimum of 10 weeks. These are cut into chops before cooking, but it is tradition not to crack the ribs. These are steamed over a rack of birch twigs for around two hours. After they are tender, they are placed under the broiler for a few minutes before serving, to make the fat crispy. *Pinnekjøtt*☆ usually is served with boiled potatoes and *kålrotstappe*☆, mashed rutabagas.

Other more unusual Christmas dinners include reindeer roast in the Lapp regions of Norway and Sweden, and boiled beef with horseradish sauce and potato pancakes in central Sweden.

Dopp i Grytan°

Dopp i grytan° is an old tradition in Sweden. The family gather around the kitchen stove to sample the cooking liquid from the Christmas ham at midday on December 24. "Dip in the Pot," as it is literally translated, requires two things—rich broth and good bread.

"DIP IN THE POT"

Stock or broth from the cooking of the Christmas ham
Beef bouillon cubes, if necessary
Sage
Soy sauce

Strain the broth from the boiled ham. Chill and remove fat from the top surface. Boil down to concentrate. Augment with bouillon, if necessary. Add sage to taste. Add soy sauce if the broth is too pale. Serve warm with *doppebröd*°.

Doppebröd°

This dark and spicy rye bread is perfect for *dopp i grytan*° on December 24. *Vörteröl*° is used in making this bread in Sweden, where it also is called *vörtlimpa*°/*vørterbrød*☆.

DIPPING BREAD

3 cakes fresh yeast
6 T. margarine
1 pint dark beer
¼ cup corn syrup
1 tsp. salt
1 tsp. ginger
1 tsp. fennel (crushed)
2 tsp. grated orange rind
6 cups or more medium
   rye flour
Around ½ cup all-pur-
   pose flour
Makes 2 loaves.

Dissolve yeast in a small amount of beer. Melt butter, add rest of beer, syrup and heat. Pour over yeast and add spices. Stir in most of the flour. Knead with more flour until smooth and elastic, around 10 minutes. Cover and let rise in a warm place until double, about 40 minutes.
Punch down and knead in rest of flour. Form two round loaves. Place on a greased baking sheet and let rise for about 30 minutes.
Preheat oven to 350°F. Bake for around 50 minutes. Brush with warm water several times while baking.

Skånsk Senap°

To many Swedes, strong Skåne mustard is the only fitting accompaniment to Christmas ham and *lutfisk*°. Real Skåne mustard is made in a wooden bowl with a cannonball to crush the mustard seeds. Skåne is the Swedish province nearest to Denmark.

SKÅNE MUSTARD

2 T. brown mustard seeds
   (available in health food
   stores)
5 tsp. water
2½ tsp. sugar
Pinch salt
2 T. whipping cream
Makes about ⅓ cup.

Crush mustard seeds with a mortar and pestle or in a blender. Add water and mix until fairly smooth. Add sugar, salt and cream and mix until evenly blended.
This mustard is very strong, so only a tiny amount is needed for each serving.

Butter Sauce

This butter sauce is a favorite accompaniment for *lutefisk*☆ in Finland.

BUTTER SAUCE

3 T. butter
2 T. all-purpose flour
1½ cups whipping cream
½ tsp. nutmeg
Makes about 1½ cups.

Melt butter over low heat and blend in flour until smooth. Add cream gradually, stirring constantly. Remove from heat and whisk in nutmeg. Pour into a sauceboat to serve.

White Sauce

Lutefisk☆ is often served with a plain bechamel, or white sauce. It is sometimes flavored with mustard.

WHITE SAUCE

2 T. butter or margarine
2 T. all-purpose flour
1¾ cups milk or light cream
Salt and pepper
1 tsp. mustard powder (optional)
Makes about 1½ cups.

Melt butter in a saucepan. Add flour, stir, and allow to cook for 1 minute. Add milk gradually, stirring constantly. Bring to a boil and let simmer for 5 minutes. Salt and pepper to taste. Stir in mustard, if desired, and cook an additional 2 minutes.

Ertestuing☆

Stewed peas are a traditional side dish for lutefisk☆. Yellow peas are preferred in certain areas, green in others.

STEWED PEAS

1¾ cups dried yellow or green peas
Water
1 tsp. salt
1 small onion, chopped
¼ bay leaf
1 tsp. sugar
1 T. butter or margarine
Serves 8.

Soak peas in cold water overnight. Discard water.
Place peas in a saucepan, add 3 cups water and 1 tsp. salt. Bring to a boil and skim. Add onion, bay leaf and sugar. Simmer, covered, for one hour or until soft. Add 1 T. butter before serving.
If there is too much liquid, make a beurre manie of 1 T. all-purpose flour and 1 T. butter or margarine and stir into mixture.

Avkokt Torsk☆

Boiled cod is the third most popular Christmas dinner in Norway, according to a survey made by an Oslo newspaper. It is served most often along the southern coast. Many people welcome this dish as a change from all the rich and heavy pork meals.

Cod is best when it is very fresh and served with the head, liver and roe, when possible. Signs at fish markets all over Norway proclaim, "*levende torsk*☆," living cod. These fish are no longer alive, but not very many hours have passed since they were.

The best cod for poaching weigh between 5 and 6 lbs. Traditionally the fish should be *rundrenset*☆, cleaned through the gills, not slit through the belly. In order to clean fish in this manner, one should cut around the gills to loosen them, and then make a slit just over the back opening, to release the insides. From the gill end, pull on the insides and remove, taking care not to break the gall bladder. Remove liver and roe, if any. Slice fish into finger-thick steaks and wash. Place fish steaks and head in cold water (add 1 T. vinegar to keep flesh firm) for at least an hour before cooking. Place liver and roe in separate bowls of cold water.

Boiled cod is really poached cod, for the water should never boil, or the fish will disintegrate. Serve this delicacy with melted butter and boiled potatoes. Garnish with parsley and lemon, if desired. *Agurksalat*☆, marinated cucumbers, is a tasty accompaniment. Unique to Norway is the custom of drinking red wine with boiled cod. It adds color to an otherwise white meal.

BOILED COD

Cod steaks
¼ cup salt for each quart water.

Bring salted water to a boil. Add cod steaks. Remove from heat and let stand for 8–10 minutes, until flesh loosens from the bone.

Transfer fish steaks to a platter, which has been spread with a linen napkin to absorb excess water.

COD LIVER

Liver from 1 cod
½ tsp. salt
1 tsp. vinegar
5 peppercorns

Remove membrane from the cod liver and place in a clean jelly jar. (Cod liver leaves an odor in the cooking utensil. Therefore, unless you have a pan especially for cooking cod liver, it is best to cook it in a jar which can be discarded after use.) Add water to cover, salt, vinegar and peppercorns. Cover with lid, but do not screw on very tightly.

Place in a pan of boiling water and cook for about 20 minutes. Serve in its own broth.

COD ROE

Wrap roe sacs in cheesecloth before cooking, as they break easily. Cook roe in lightly salted water for about 15 minutes. Serve warm with fish.

Agurksalat☆

Very few salads were included in the Christmas menues of the past, because fresh vegetables, other than rutabaga, cabbage, carrots and potatoes, were not available. Many families today, however, serve a marinated cucumber salad with boiled cod and other fresh fish.

CUCUMBER SALAD

1 cucumber, preferably
the long, thin variety

DRESSING:
3 T. white vinegar
3 T. water
1 T. sugar
Salt and pepper
Chopped parsley
(optional)
Serves 4.

Peel cucumber and slice thinly (an *ostehøvel*☆, cheese slicer, does this beautifully. Mix dressing and pour over cucumber slices. Chill for at least one hour before serving. Garnish with chopped parsley.

Ribbe*

*Ribbe** is fresh bacon with the ribs and sometimes even the chops still attached. The traditional Christmas *ribbe** dinner also includes *medisterpølser**, pork sausages, and *medisterkaker**, cakes of spiced ground pork. This is the simplest recipe for *ribbe**, but it is one which lies dear to the heart of many a Norwegian.

ROAST WHOLE BACON

3 lbs. whole fresh bacon with bones and rind (Ask butcher to crack the bones at 3–4" intervals.)

2 tsp. salt

½ tsp. pepper

1 tsp. dry mustard, (optional)

Serves 8 with sausages and meat cakes.

Rub meat with salt and pepper (and mustard) and refrigerate for 1–3 days. Cut a diamond pattern in the rind and lay *ribbe**, rind side down, in cold water for 2 hours—this makes it extra crunchy. Preheat oven to 350°F.

Place *ribbe**, rind side up, on a rack in a roasting pan, and pour 1 cup water in the bottom. Roast for 1½ to 2 hours. If the rind is still not crunchy enough, place under the broiler for a few minutes before serving, making sure that it does not burn. About 20 minutes before serving, pour off juices, skim and make a gravy, if desired—the concentrated juices are delicious alone, and add pork sausages and cakes to heat.

Medisterkaker*

These ground pork cakes are eaten year-round in Norway, but they have a special place on the Christmas Eve table. A special ground meat mixture for these is sold at many meat counters. *Medisterpølser**, pork sausages, are made from basically the same mixture, only more finely ground.

Americans are taught to handle ground meat as little as possible. Just the opposite is true in Scandinavia for many recipes. Ground meat (usually more finely ground than ours) is mixed thoroughly with salt and flour, so that the meat will absorb liquid and stretch. The consistency of this extended meat mixture is fluffy and of an even color, rather like pink mashed potatoes. The finished product has a bouncy, porous texture.

SAUSAGE CAKES

1 lb. finely ground pork
1½ tsp. salt
½ tsp. pepper
¼ tsp. ginger
⅛ tsp. nutmeg
1 T. all purpose flour or potato flour
Up to ¾ cup milk or bouillon to moisten
Oil or other fat for frying

Serves 4 without any other meat dishes, serves 8 with ribbe☆.

Mix meat, seasonings and flour well. Add liquid gradually, mixing well. Form flattened meatballs.

Brown on both sides before placing alongside ribbe☆. Bake with ribbe☆ for 20 minutes.

Surkål☆

Germans seafarers brought sauerkraut to Norway during the Hanseatic period. This is a caraway-flavored variation, which is eaten with the Christmas ribbe☆ and with other pork dishes the rest of the year.

NORWEGIAN SAUERKRAUT

1 head cabbage (about 2 lbs.), shredded
2–3 T. oil or other fat
2 cups stock or water
2 T. all-purpose flour
2 tsp. salt
2 tsp. caraway seed
1 sour apple, peeled and sliced
1½ tsp. vinegar
2 tsp. sugar
Serves 8.

Heat oil or melt fat. Add cabbage, stock or water, flour, salt, caraway seed and apple. Cover and simmer for about 1 hour, adding additional liquid, if necessary. Add sugar and vinegar 5 minutes before serving.

Långkål[◇]

Braised whole kale is another traditional accompaniment to the Christmas ham. It has long been considered one of Denmark's national specialties and is often served with roast duck.

BRAISED WHOLE KALE

2 whole kale stalks
Ham stock, or broth from
  cooking sylte[☆], head
  cheese
2 T. butter
Salt and pepper
Serves 6–8

Remove the toughest and coarsest parts of the kale and rinse thoroughly. Simmer in broth until tender, approximately 30 minutes. Drain well. Melt butter and brown kale well. Salt and pepper to taste.

Stuffed Pork Loin

The Danish Christmas table often features a pork loin roast served with the same accompaniments as goose, pickled red cabbage and sugar-glazed potatoes.

STUFFED PORK LOIN

Around 12 pitted prunes
¾ cup dry white wine
4 lb. boneless pork loin
  roast
1 tsp. salt
¼ tsp. pepper
1 tsp. ginger
1 tart apple, peeled, cored
  and sliced
1–2 T. all-purpose flour
¾ cup light cream
1 T. red currant jelly
Serves 6–8.

Soak prunes in wine for 2 hours.
Preheat oven to 325°F. Make a hole through the center of the roast. Season meat with salt, pepper and ginger. Mix prunes and apple slices and stuff roast, using the handle of a wooden spoon to push the mixture into place. Bind and tie roast well, so that it will retain its shape. Roast for about 2 hours, or until meat thermometer indicates roast is done. Remove to a serving platter and allow to rest 10 minutes before carving.
Sprinkle flour over drippings. Whisk in wine and cream, stirring up all bits adhering to the bottom. Cook for 5 minutes. Stir in jelly and heat thoroughly. Pour sauce into a gravy boat and serve with the meat.

Brunkål°

"Brown cabbage" is made from white cabbage which has been braised in stock to a rich brown color. It is a traditional accompaniment for the Christmas ham, but it tastes good year-round.

BRAISED CABBAGE

1 head cabbage (around
    4 lbs.)
3 apples
¼ cup oil or other fat for
    cooking
½–⅔ cup bouillon or stock
2 tsp. salt
3 T. light brown sugar
2 T. vinegar
Serves 8.

Shred cabbage and apple and brown in oil, stirring often. Add stock, cover, and let simmer on low heat until tender, about 30–40 minutes. Stir in salt, sugar and vinegar. Heat thoroughly before serving.

Creamed Kale

Creamed kale is similar to creamed spinach in method of preparation. Spinach is popular in Scandinavia, but it is available only in limited quantities, and even today, fresh spinach is a seasonal vegetable. Frozen spinach is available year-round, and can be substituted for kale in some recipes.

CREAMED KALE

1½ lbs. fresh kale, or one
    package frozen
1½ T. butter or margarine
2 T. all-purpose flour
1 cup milk
Salt and pepper
Pinch sugar
Pinch nutmeg
Serves 6.

Clean and rinse kale, discarding stalks and heavy ribs.

Cook until tender in lightly salted water, around 15 minutes. Drain well and chop. If using frozen kale, follow directions on the package.

Melt butter, add flour and cook for one minute. Add milk gradually, stirring constantly and bring to a boil. Add salt, pepper, sugar and nutmeg and cook for three minutes. Add chopped kale and heat thoroughly.

Gåsestek°

What could be more majestic than roast goose? Many people are afraid to prepare it, but it is not difficult at all. Goose has a heavy carcass, so a 12 lb. goose will not serve more than 10. Traditional accompaniments for roast goose are pickled red cabbage and sugar-glazed potatoes. It is the most popular Christmas dinner in Germany as well as in Denmark.

Duck can be prepared in the same way. A 4½ lb. duck serves 4 and takes about 1½ hours to roast.

ROAST GOOSE

1 goose (around 12 lbs.)
½ lemon
Salt and pepper

STOCK:
Giblets and wing tips
½ carrot
1 small onion, quartered
1 stalk celery, in 2"
* lengths*
1 tsp. salt
¼ tsp. pepper
¼ tsp. thyme

STUFFING:
As many apples as there
* are people*
Pitted prunes

SAUCE:
About 3 cups goose stock
* (augment with chicken*
* bouillon, if necessary)*
½ cup port wine
Salt and pepper
¼ cup all-purpose flour
¼ cup butter
Serves 8–10.

Clean goose well—be sure to remove any bloody bits from the cavity, as it will be stuffed. Reserve liver for another use. Cut off wing tips at outer joint for stock pot. Rinse goose inside and out. Dry with paper towels. Squeeze lemon inside the cavity.

Place stock ingredients in a large saucepan and add water to cover. Bring to a boil, skim and simmer until tender.

Preheat oven to 425°F.

Pare and core apples and stuff with prunes. Place apples and any additional prunes inside the cavity. Secure with skewers at both ends. Use a skewer to prick the entire bird at close intervals for the fat to drain off. Roast goose, breast side up for 20 minutes. Pour off fat. (This fat is marvelous for making pickled red cabbage, and for frying.)

Lower temperature to 350°F, and continue roasting for 3 to 3½ hours, basting occasionally with stock. Pour off fat as necessary. Turn goose several times while roasting, so that it can brown on all sides. Roast with breast up for the last 20 minutes. Remove goose to a serving platter and allow to rest for 10 minutes before carving.

Skim as much fat as possible from the roasting pan, and add stock, scraping up all bits from the bottom. Add wine and cook for 5 minutes. Skim. Make *beurre manie* of butter and flour and whisk into pan. Allow to thicken, add salt and pepper to taste. Pour into a gravy boat. Remove apples and prunes from the cavity and serve with the goose.

Rødkål°

No Christmas goose is complete without pickled red cabbage. Serve this tasty vegetable with roast duck or pork all year.

PICKLED RED CABBAGE

1 head red cabbage (about 2 lbs.), shredded.
3 T. oil or other fat (rendered poultry fat is best)
2 T. chopped onion
¼ cup sugar
1 T. vinegar
1 T. salt
1 small apple, peeled, cored and sliced
1 tsp. caraway seed
Red wine or water, if necessary
Serves 8.

Brown onion and sugar in oil. Add cabbage, and sprinkle with vinegar and salt. Add caraway seed and apple. Simmer, covered, for 1 hour or more, until tender. Add additional liquid if cabbage dries out.

Brunede Kartofler°

These sugar-glazed potatoes are the traditional Danish accompaniment for roast goose or duck.

SUGAR-GLAZED POTATOES

18 small potatoes, all of similar size
6–7 T. sugar
6 T. butter
Serves 6.

Boil potatoes in their jackets until just cooked through. Peel.
Melt butter and sugar in a frying pan, stirring constantly. When the sugar is completely melted and begins to turn a light brown, add half of the potatoes and roll to coat. When these are coated, remove and add the rest. Serve immediately.

Pinnekjøtt☆

Pinnekjøtt☆ is a Christmas dish which is most popular along the West Coast of Norway. It is made from year-old lamb, which is drysalted and hung to dry for at least 10 weeks. After drying, it is lightly smoked. It is traditionally cooked on a bed of birch twigs to add extra flavor. Accompaniments are mashed rutabagas and boiled potatoes. If there is a Scandinavian delicatessen near your home, you may be able to get *pinnekjøtt*☆.

PINNEKJØTT

5–6 lbs. pinnekjøtt☆
Serves 8–10

Cut meat into chops, but do not crack ribs. Soak in cold water for at least 6 hours.
Place birch twigs (without bark) on a metal rack in the bottom of a heavy pot. Pour water up to the level of the rack. Distribute meat evenly on the rack and steam for around 2½ hours or until tender. Do not allow water to touch meat. Serve hot on heated plates (lamb fat congeals quickly) with mashed rutabagas, boiled potatoes and mustard.

Kålrotstappe*

The rutabaga is a staple vegetable in Scandinavia, because this hardy variety of turnip grows well in the northern latitudes. It is equally tasty warm as puree and cold in slaw. Because of its high level of vitamin C, it is called the "orange of the north." Mashed rutabaga is the traditional accompaniment for *pinnekjøtt**.

MASHED RUTABAGA

1 rutabaga (around 1¾ lbs.)
3–4 small potatoes
⅓ cup milk
2–3 T. butter or margarine
Salt and pepper
Serves 8.

Peel and slice rutabaga and potatoes. Boil together in lightly salted water until soft. Drain and mash. Add milk and butter and beat until smooth. Add salt and pepper to taste.

The Peace
of Christmas

Old Nordic church laws state that *julefred*, the peace of Christmas, should last from the first Sunday in Advent until January 13. During the Middle Ages this was shortened, and in Denmark and Sweden the peace of Christmas began on December 25 and in Norway on December 21. It lasted until January 6 in Denmark and until January 13 in Norway and Sweden.

Peace reigned for all God's creatures, and no hunting or fishing was allowed. Modern game laws still respect this. People committing violent crimes during the peace of Christmas were punished doubly hard, for they were not only breaking the rules of society, but blaspheming the Lord as well.

For the last 100 years or so, Christmas officially has begun with the ringing of church bells on Christmas Eve, and with this signal the peace of Christmas begins. At some remote farms, where the church bells could not be heard, it was customary to fire a shot at sunset to initiate the holiday festivities. This shot served a dual purpose—it marked the holiday and it scared away the evil spirits who were thought to be especially threatening on Christmas Eve.

Because of the demands of modern life, Christmas peace really lasts only from sunset on Christmas Eve through December 26, which is a holiday in Scandinavia.

Merry Christmas 1881 by Olaf M. Olsen. This series of vignettes shows many aspects of a Norwegian Christmas. From the top: The ringing of the church bell calls the people to worship. A city family enjoy the "living lights" on the Christmas tree. The women's clothing and the large curtained window indicate an urban setting. A *stabbur* or storage house and a barn are set slightly apart from the main farm dwelling. Pigs are slaughtered for the Christmas menu, and a well-dressed *nisse* enjoys a tankard of beer, with the kegs in the background. Country folk dance to the music of a fiddler at a *julestue*. A *nisse* finishes his porridge, and a sheaf of grain is placed against the rood of the barn. The whole picture is joined together by the stylized dragon heads of the church portal, the rood of the barn and the lower framework, a popular design element of the late 19th century in Scandinavia.

Glædelig Jul.

1881

Christmas Tree

For most people Christmas is unthinkable without a tree, and dancing and singing around the *juletre*☆/*julgran*○/*juletræ*◇, are a beloved part of the Scandinavian Christmas tradition. The Christmas tree, however, is still relatively new to Scandinavia and has enjoyed widespread acceptance only in the last 100 years. Many 19th century theologians were against the Christmas tree, because they were afraid that it, rather than the Christ child, would become the center of the celebration. Even at the turn of this century people in the more remote areas regarded the Christmas tree with skepticism.

Decorating the house with green branches has long been a part of the Christmas celebration throughout Scandinavia, but they do not seem to have any connection with the Christmas tree. These branches were placed at the entrance to the house or barn—the sharp needles would keep evil from entering. Sometimes these branches were formed into a cross to get a combined effect.

The Christmas tree came to Scandinavia from central Europe. It is interesting to note that in pre-Christian times, the oak tree was the holy plant of northern Europe and was known as Odin's tree. But in the 8th century, St. Boniface dedicated the fir tree to Christ to symbolize the survival of Christianity. Although the Catholics sometimes used the tree, it was the Protestants of southwest Germany and Switzerland who adopted it as part of the home feast of Christmas sometime in the 16th century. The custom of St. Nicholas bringing gifts to children on December 6 was transferred to the Christmas tree as bearer of gifts, for small parcels were hung on its branches. An angel symbolizing the Christ child was placed on top to signify that he was the true bearer of the presents. Later, as the *nisse*☆/*tomte*○ (See *nisse*☆/*tomte*○, Page 00.) took over the role of gift giver, the angel was replaced with a star. By the end of the 18th century the Christmas tree had reached Denmark, where it first was accepted by the upper classes in Copenhagen. It was introduced to the countryside by teachers and the clergy through *juletræfester*°/*juletrefester*☆, Christmas tree parties for children.

Fir trees are not plentiful in Denmark, and the first Christmas trees usually were small and were placed on a table. In bourgeois homes the trees were decorated with dried fruit, apples, gingerbread, candy in paper wrappers and sometimes garlands of raisins or small gifts. Small candles were attached to the ends of the branches, though they seldom were lit except for a few minutes on Christmas Eve and maybe on Christmas day. Decorations were simpler in rural homes.

Fir trees are plentiful in most parts of rural Norway and Sweden, and the size of tree usually was determined by the amount of space in the living room. The Christmas tree was traditionally brought home from the woods by father and the children. In some places trees were hung from the ceiling over the Christmas table, because there was very little floor space in these small dwellings. This was practical, too, for the trees' decorations were protected from the small hands of the younger members of the household.

Artificial trees of wood also were used throughout Scandinavia and may even predate the live fir tree. These were most common in Denmark and Sweden. These *julepyramider*°, Christmas pyramids, or *äppelträder*°, appletrees, are believed to be of German origin. They were made of a central post with many sidearms projecting from it. In Denmark the projections were hung with fir branches, while in Sweden, they usually were carved and decorated with flowers and hearts and painted in red, green and gold. All were equipped with candleholders and sticks for apples, in remembrance of the legend that apple trees blossomed in their joy at the birth of Jesus. Apples were a treat at Christmas, and in some places they were the children's only gifts.

In 1914 the first outdoor Christmas tree in Scandinavia was lit in Copenhagen at the town hall square. This custom has spread to the other large cities and towns of Scandinavia, but it is still unusual for families to decorate their outdoor trees or their houses with lights.

Today Christmas trees are the focal point of the celebration of Christmas in the home throughout Scandinavia. *Furu*☆, pine, and *gran*☆, spruce, are the most common varieties, with the shortneedled *gran*☆ the favorite. The Swedish word for Christmas tree, *julgran*°, makes no mistake of that. Most Scandinavians feel that the tree itself is just as important as the decorations, and most trees are rather sparsely decorated by American standards. The trees are still hung with gingerbread and candy in heart-shaped baskets. Small artificial

apples have replaced the real ones of times past, but ornaments of *halm*⁎ and *spon*⁎ (wood shavings) hearken back to a bygone era. The heart, symbol of Christian love, appears in many forms of tree decorations. Unique to Scandinavia are the garlands of national flags which are strung vertically on the tree. Hans Christian Anderson mentions these flags in several of his Christmas stories. The origin of this custom is uncertain, but the flags probably became popular during the last century and the beginning of the present, when national identity and patriotism became important to Scandinavians. This is especially true for Norway, which became independent from Sweden in 1905. Christmas tree lights are always white and are often in the form of electric candles. The tree is placed in the center of the room, so that it can be seen from all angles and can be encircled easily for the singing and dancing which are so important to the celebration of Christmas.

Marsipan⁎

Marzipan can be bought readymade all over Scandinavia and in the U.S. at specialty shops. If you cannot get marzipan, you can make it from scratch. Children love to make marzipan figures.

MARZIPAN

1 cup blanched almonds *1 cup confectioner's sugar* *½ egg white* *1–2 tsp. cold water* *½ tsp. almond flavoring* Makes about 1¾ cups.	Grind almonds as finely as possible and blend with sugar. Add egg white and water. Knead until smooth.

The Christmas Holiday by F. G. Nordmann. The Christ Child is at the center of this picture, against a background of the Christmas star and a candle-lit tree. The Christ Child appears as the bearer of gifts, as in earlier German tradition. His hands direct the viewer to the gifts on either side, a basket of apples, a toy goat and many other playthings. On the right, a woman has adorned the grave of a departed loved one with a wreath. Below, the church is lit to receive worshippers at Christmas. Even though the artist is called Nordmann, which means "Norwegian," the picture has a distinct north German flavor in the dominance of the Christ Child over the entire composition and in the scene with the wreath. The church has more leaded glass than was the usual in Norway and Sweden at that time.

Nisse / Tomte

Perhaps the best known and most popular figure of Christmas lore in Scandinavia is the *nisse*✩/*tomte*○ sometimes even called *tomtenisse*✩.

The *julenisse*✩, or *jultomte*○, is a blend of St. Nicholas and the *nisse*✩/*tomte*○ of Scandinavian folk tradition. It is coincidental that *nisse*✩ is a nickname for Nils, which is derived from Nicholas.

St. Nicholas was a bishop in Asia Minor in the 4th century. As patron saint of children, he was supposed to give small presents to good children and rods to lazy ones on December 6, his feast day. He became so popular that he survived the Reformation and is a part of the Christmas tradition in most countries, although the date of his appearance has been transferred to December 24 or 25 in most places. The English and German Father Christmas, Santa Claus and to some degree the modern Scandinavian gift-bringing *julenisse*✩/*jultomte*○ are his descendants.

The *nisse*✩/*tomte*○ originated in the housegods of pre-Christian times. When Christianity spread throughout Europe, worship of these housegods was discontinued, but the belief that every home had a small supernatural being as its protector survived, especially in Scandinavia. The name of this figure varied from place to place. He was called *gårdboen*◇ in Denmark, *gardvorden*✩ or *tunvorden*✩ in Norway, and *tomtegubbe*○ or *tomtekarl*○ in Sweden. *Gårdboen*◇ means farm inhabitant; *gardvorden*✩ means farm protector and a *tun*✩ is a grouping of farm buildings; *tomtegubbe*○ means an old man who belongs to a lot on which there are buildings, and *karl*○ is another word for man. Thus the *nisse*✩/*tomte*○ was a little man who belonged to the land on which the farm was built and he most often remained there, even if the owner moved. He could move if he chose, but he rarely did, for he was thought to be descended from the original inhabitant of the farm.

The *nisse*✩/*tomte*○ was a rather temperamental, easily offended little man who kept strict order on the farm as long as the resident family

Julemannen◇, The Danish version of Father Christmas, traditionally brings the Christmas tree along with the presents. Note the birch rods in his pocket for the naughty children.

took good care of him. The success or failure of the farm was his responsibility, and he was the protector of all the buildings and the animals. He worked year-round and was a kind of security factor for the farm family. It was important to insure oneself for the next harvest, and it was not worth the risk to offend the *nisse*☆/*tomte*○. If he were insulted, he could take revenge on the family—he could even disappear and take the happiness of the farm with him. On Christmas Eve he was rewarded with a bowl of porridge with a large lump of butter in it, plus a *skål*☆ or saucer of beer, although some families fed their little protector more regularly. If he were dissatisfied with the food, he threw it against the wall. The next evening he was usually given finer porridge with an even bigger lump of butter and perhaps some *lefse*☆ to placate him. On Christmas morning, the children of the household ran to the barn to see if the *nisse*☆/*tomte*○ had enjoyed his meal. The bowl was usually licked clean, thanks to some four-legged friend. Many folk songs tell about the *nisse*☆/*tomte*○ eating his porridge in the barn while the cat and mice watch.

The *nisse*☆/*tomte*○ usually worked invisibly, but occasionally one caught a glimpse of him in the shadows. He was about the size of a five-year-old and wore a grey tunic, a red stocking cap, and usually wooden clogs. He was very old and had a long white beard. Sometimes he smoked a pipe. He usually lived alone in the barn, but on some farms there were several *nisser*☆/*tomter*○. Occasionally he was known to take a wife.

When the story of St. Nicholas the gift-giver came to Scandinavia, it was well suited to the *nisser*☆/*tomter*○ who always had been around. This was just another job for them to do. By 1850 the custom of the *nisse*☆ bringing gifts was well established in Denmark, owing to the popular literature of the time. He reached the people of rural Scandinavia in much the same way as the Christmas tree, via the bourgeoisie and the schools. But in some places as late as the turn of this century, children were afraid to see the *nisse*☆/*tomte*○ in the house, for they knew that his place was in the barn and that he was not very fond of children.

It was really the artists of the late 19th century who created the present day picture of the *nisse*☆/*tomte*○. Pictures of gift-giving *nisser*☆/*tomter*○ first appeared on Christmas cards and in special Christmas magazines toward the end of the 19th century. Jenny Nyström, a Swedish card and book illustrator whose voluminous production spanned from 1875 into the 1930's, was probably the most instrumental single person in establishing the identity of the contemporary

At Christmastime by Jenny Nyström. Two children serve a bowl of porridge to the *tomte*° on their farm.

nisse☆/*tomte*○. Her *tomter*○ are jolly little men in grey tunics and red stocking caps sporting long beards and broad smiles. They look rather like older versions of Santa's helpers. They often appear in groups and take part in all aspects of the Christmas celebration. Reproductions of Jenny Nyström's *tomter*○ are among the best-selling Christmas cards in Scandinavia today.

The *nisse*☆/*tomte*○ appears just after dinner on Christmas Eve in every household with children. *"Er det noen snille barn her?"*☆ "Are there any good children here?" he asks, and then he opens his sack of gifts. He still bears some relation to St. Nicholas with his long red robe, but his jolly demeanor is more like our own Santa Claus.

Risengrynsgrøt☆/Risgrynsgröt○

Generations ago, the surprises in the rice porridge were supposed to predict one's marital future: A sweet almond meant marriage within the year; a bitter almond indicated bachelorhood/spinsterhood; a brown bean signified marriage with a widower or a widow with five children (!); and a metal ring predicted an engagement. Today we remember this old tradition by placing a sweet almond in the porridge, and the person finding it gets a marzipan pig.

Rice porridge should be made with round or short grain rice. For best results, do not use converted rice.

RICE PORRIDGE

1 cup rice
1 cup water
1 T. butter
1 large piece stick cinnamon
1½ tsp. salt
4 cups milk ½ cup heavy cream (or more milk)
1 blanched almond
Cinnamon, sugar, cold milk for serving
Serves 6.

Wash rice in a sieve under cold running water.
Bring water, butter, cinnamon and salt to a boil and add rice. Cook, uncovered, over medium heat until the water has disappeared, stirring frequently. Add milk and simmer, covered, on lowest possible heat until rice is tender and milk is absorbed. Remove from heat and stir in heavy cream and the almond.
Transfer porridge to a serving dish and sprinkle with cinnamon and sugar. Serve with a pitcher of cold milk.

Gifts

Gifts have long been associated with Christmas, but until the last few generations they were simple, practical and homemade. They were usually articles of clothing which people needed. On Barbara's day, December 4, housewives would begin to spin, weave and knit for Christmas. Socks and mittens were the most popular gifts.

Servants were given bread, liquor and clothing at Christmas, but these gifts were really part of their salary which was distributed at Christmas. The clergy and other "professionals" such as the blacksmith or midwife also received similar gifts, but these too could be considered pay for services rendered.

Charity was important at Christmas, and those who could afford it were expected to help the needy. In some areas the poor went from farm to farm collecting gifts of food, candles and coins. In other places the farmers visited needy families on Christmas Eve. Sometimes the poor did small services in return for the gifts they received. A modern Christmas charity, which originated in Denmark in 1904, is the Christmas seal to help needy or sick children. Many other countries have adopted this custom.

Gifts for children other than clothing were uncommon before the introduction of the Christmas tree, although in central Europe children received gifts on St. Nicholas' day, December 6. The clergy stressed that it was blasphemous to celebrate the birth of the Christ child by spoiling one's own children, so the first gifts were simple, usually some Christmas cookies or other special foods. In Hardanger, Norway, children were given an apple as their Christmas gift in the late 19th century. After the tree became popular, children's gifts were tiny parcels or sweets which hung from its branches. It was not until this century that most gifts were wrapped and placed under the tree, and it is only a recent tradition that children give presents to their parents.

Since the beginning of the tradition of gift-giving by the Romans on New Year's day, gifts generally were presented by high status people

Christmas Eve, drawing by Jenny Nyström, engraving by J. Engberg. Christmas gifts are being delivered by a team of hardworking *tomter.*° The ringing of the church bell and the placement of a sheaf of grain for the birds mark the beginning of the holiday.

to those below them. It was not until the end of the 18th century that gifts were exchanged among equals. During the rise of the bourgeoisie, gift-giving became more popular and developed into an art.

In Scandinavia, most gifts were presented anonymously—someone knocked on the door, threw the gifts into the house and ran as fast as he could. The Swedish word for Christmas present, *julklapp*°, Christmas knock, derives from this practice. These small packages were accompanied by short, often humorous, verses. The young people of the household often went to great lengths to catch the person distributing gifts. A similar tradition existed in England until around 200 years ago, in which an unknown person stood behind a door and threw straw figures to the children of the household.

The first gift wrap in Scandinavia appeared around the turn of the century. *Glanspapir*☆, shiny paper, was printed in bright solid colors on shiny white paper. It was very expensive, but it soon became popular. It is still produced today, not for wrapping packages, but for making the woven hearts and other paper ornaments which decorate most Scandinavian Christmas trees.

Mjuk Pepparkaka°

This is a lovely moist Swedish spice cake flavored with lingonberry jam. It keeps well and makes a lovely homemade gift.

SWEDISH SPICE CAKE

1 egg
1 cup sugar
1 tsp. ginger
1 tsp. cinnamon
½ tsp. cloves
¼ cup lingonberry jam (other tart jam can be substituted)
¼ cup melted butter or margarine
⅔ cup sour cream or sour half and half
1 tsp. baking soda
1⅓ cups all-purpose flour
Makes 1 loaf.

Preheat oven to 375°F.
Beat egg and sugar until lemon colored. Add spices, jam, melted butter and sour cream. Stir in soda and flour. Pour into a greased and floured 8½ × 4½ × 2½" loaf pan and bake around 40 minutes. Cool for 5 minutes before removing from pan.

Limpa°

Swedish rye bread is dark and delicious. It is usually round, always flavored with orange rind or fennel. This bread has an especially lovely texture and a well-developed flavor, if it is allowed to rise for a third time.

SWEDISH RYE BREAD

2 packages active dry yeast
1½ cups warm water
¼ cup light molasses
⅓ cup sugar
2 tsp. salt
2 T. margarine
3 T. grated orange rind or
  1 tsp. fennel
2½ cups medium rye flour
2½ cups all-purpose flour
4 T. farina
Makes 2 loaves.

Soften yeast in warm water in a large mixing bowl. Stir in molasses, sugar, salt, margarine and orange rind or fennel. Stir in rye flour and beat until smooth. Add enough all-purpose flour to make a soft dough, reserving some for kneading. Turn out onto a floured board, cover and let rest for 10 minutes.

Knead until smooth and elastic, about 10 minutes. Place in greased bowl, and turn greased side up. Cover and let rise in a warm place until double, about 1 hour.

Punch dough down. Divide into 2 parts and form 2 round, rather flat loaves. Place on opposite corners of a cookie sheet which has been greased and sprinkled with farina. Cover and let rise again until double, about 1 hour.

Preheat oven to 375°F. Bake 30–35 minutes.

Glasmästersill°

"Glazier's herring" is always made in a glass container, so that the beautiful colors of the ingredients can be seen, thus its name. It is never made with filets. Put it in a pretty jar, tie a ribbon around it and give as a Christmas gift.

"GLAZIER'S HERRING"

2 salt herrings, cleaned
   and soaked—do not
   filet or skin. (See Notes
   on Herring, Page 137.)
½ carrot, sliced
1–2 red onions, sliced
1 piece fresh horseradish,
   peeled and finely diced
1 T. pickling spice
2 bay leaves
½ cup vinegar
½ cup water
¼ cup sugar

Makes 10–12 buffet-style
servings.

Cut herring into 1″ lengths and layer with
vegetables and spices in a glass jar.
Bring vinegar, water and sugar to a boil.
Cool, and pour over herring. All herring
must be covered with brine. Chill, covered, for 2–4 days before serving.

Portvinsild☆

Herring in port wine is a modern Christmas recipe. Put this in a fancy
container and you have a delicious gift, if you are invited to someone's
house during the holiday season.

PORT WINE HERRING

4 salt herrings, cleaned,
   soaked, fileted and
   skinned (See Notes on
   Herring, Page 137.)
¾ cup vinegar
½ cup sugar
3 T. oil
⅓ cup port wine
1 medium onion, sliced
1 tsp. sage

Makes 16–20 buffet-style
servings.

Cut herring into 1″ pieces and place with
onion in a jar. Mix vinegar, sugar, oil, port
and sage and pour over herring.
Refrigerate, covered, for at least 24 hours
before serving.

The First Day of Christmas

Early on Christmas morning, the host and hostess went around to everyone staying in the house with food and drink, usually *vørterbrød*[☆]/ *vörtlimpor*[○] and beer, which more recently has been replaced with coffee. Even the servants were served. No one was allowed to sleep late on this day, or else he would be drowsy for the rest of the year.

After they finished eating this breakfast, the family took the horse and sleigh to church for early morning services, called *julottan*[○] in Sweden. These sometimes began as early as 4 a.m., although 7 or 8 a.m. was more usual. The men carried torches to light the way to church. These were thrown on the ground in front of the church to make a great bonfire.

The dead were thought to hold services at midnight, so it was important not to arrive at church too early for fear of disturbing them. Before sitting down, churchgoers wiped off the pews, so that no dust from the dead remained.

After church services were over people raced home, for the first family to arrive back home would be the first to harvest its crops in the fall. Some people went to great lengths to win the race—they even enlisted the help of the resident *nisse*[☆]/*tomte*[○]. A pot of hot mulled wine, *gløgg*[☆], was waiting for them at home, because they often were chilled to the bone after services in an unheated church and the ride home with the wind howling about them.

December 25 was a day of rest and everyone stayed at home, for it was considered an insult to the spirit of Christmas to go out. Only the most vital tasks were performed and no food was prepared. Dinner from *julaften*[☆] was still on the table and there was plenty of food for everyone.

This cold table of food on Christmas morning is the ancestor of the

Christmas by Jenny Nyström. Going to church by torchlight early on Christmas morning.

julefrokost☆/*julfrokost*○ which is so popular throughout Scandinavia today. In fact, this meal is the most important of the entire holiday in Denmark, and the Danes do have a great reputation for making lavish cold tables. The modern Christmas breakfast table is laden with cold ham, various kinds of herring, salads, liver pate, Christmas cheese, usually Edam with its festive red wax covering, plus several kinds of bread. At many homes guests are invited to enjoy this delightful meal, which can extend well into the afternoon.

Svensk Skinke°

The Swedish Christmas ham is first served on Christmas Day, although its broth has been tasted in *dopp i grytan°* at lunch on Christmas Eve. This is a lightly salted, lightly smoked ham, which is very similar to our own hams. Buy a bone-in ham and follow your usual method of preparation, or that recommended by your butcher—he knows how long it has to soak, or whether soaking is even necessary. Do not glaze, for it is the special mustard and crumb topping which gives Swedish ham its identity.

MUSTARD-CRUMB TOPPING FOR SWEDISH BAKED HAM

5 T. Swedish-style or other dark mustard
3 T. Dijon-style mustard
1 T. potato starch or cornstarch
1 egg
1 tsp. oil
Dry breadcrumbs
Whole cloves

Makes enough topping for 1 large ham.

After the ham is baked, remove rind and score fat.
Heat oven to 450°F.
Mix together both mustards, starch, egg and oil. Spread mixture on ham. Sprinkle with crumbs and decorate with cloves. Bake for 15 minutes. Let ham rest a few minutes before slicing.

Kylling Sylte☆

If the thought of making a traditional *sylte*☆ scares you, or if you are watching your cholesterol intake, this chicken version is just the thing. It is low in calories and is a perfect alternative to the many heavy dishes served at Christmas.

CHICKEN SYLTE

2 broiler-fryers (around 2 or 2½ lbs. each)

SALT BRINE:
3 quarts water
⅔ cup salt

Make the brine by dissolving ⅔ cup salt in 3 quarts water in a deep, but not wide pot.
Clean and rinse chickens and place in brine. Weigh them down, so they are completely covered. Store in a cold place for around 1½ days.

FOR COOKING:
Water
2 bay leaves
2 tsp. whole black
  peppercorns
1 carrot
the green part of a leek

FOR ASPIC:
3 cups chicken broth
¼ tsp. thyme
⅛ tsp. ground white
  pepper
1 T. gelatin powder
Serves 8, 16 if buffet-style.

Remove chickens from brine and place in stewing pot. Add just enough water to cover. Bring to a boil, skim and add bay leaves, peppercorns, carrot and leek. Simmer, covered, for about 45 minutes. Remove chickens from broth and let cool, but continue cooking broth, uncovered. Skin and bone chickens. Return bones to broth. Reduce broth to 3 cups.

Cut chicken into small pieces and place in a large saucepan. Strain broth and pour over meat. Add thyme and white pepper and bring to a boil.

Soften gelatin in a small amount of cold water. Dissolve in a little broth and add to saucepan with chicken.

Pour into a 5–6 cup mold and chill to stiffen. Chicken *sylte*☆ can be frozen, but it must be brought to the boiling point and remolded before serving.

Sursild☆

This is the most popular variety of marinated herring in Norway. You can make it more festive by adding chopped red and green pepper as well as onion.

MARINATED HERRING

2 salt herrings, cleaned, soaked, fileted and skinned (See Notes on Herring, Page 137.)
1 onion, sliced
1 bay leaf
1 T. pickling spice
⅓ cup vinegar
½ cup water
⅓ cup sugar
1 T. chopped leek or chives
Makes 10–12 buffet-style servings.

Cut herring into 1″ pieces and layer with onion slices and pickling spice in a jar. Place bay leaf on top.

Bring vinegar, sugar and water to a boil. Cool and pour over herring. Chill for at least 24 hours before serving

Kryddsill°

Spiced herring is a classic among Swedish herring dishes. Those who appreciate spicy dishes will love *kryddsill.*°

SPICED HERRING

4 salt herrings, cleaned, soaked, fileted and skinned (See Notes on Herring, Page 137.)
30 allspice berries
30 black peppercorns
10 cloves
2 or 3 bay leaves
¾ cup chopped red onion
1 tsp. yellow mustard seed
6 T. wine vinegar
6 T. warm water
6 T. sugar

Makes 16–20 buffet-style servings

Pound allspice, pepper and cloves in a mortar. Cut herring into 1″ pieces and layer with onion, bay leaves, mustard seed and spices in a serving bowl.

Dissolve sugar in warm water and add vinegar. Pour brine over herring, cover and refrigerate for at least 12 hours before serving. *Kryddsill*° will keep for around 5 days in the refrigerator.

Sillsallad°

This is the traditional herring salad found on all Swedish Christmas tables.

HERRING SALAD

1 large salt herring, cleaned, soaked, fileted and skinned (See Notes on Herring, page 137.)
6 pickled beets
3 boiled potatoes
2 apples
1 small onion, minced
2 dill pickles
½ cup diced roast veal or pork
½ cup diced tongue or corned beef

Cut all ingredients into small dice and mix together with dressing. Pack into a decorative mold and refrigerate for at least 3 hours.

Turn out onto a platter and garnish with sliced egg.

DRESSING:
- 1 T. Swedish-style mustard
- 1 tsp. dark Dijon-style mustard
- 1 T. sugar
- 2 T. vinegar
- 3 T. vegetable oil
- ¼ cup whipped cream

2 hard-boiled eggs for garnish

Makes 10–12 buffet-style servings.

Dressing: Blend both mustards, add sugar and vinegar. Slowly add oil, stirring constantly. Fold in whipped cream.

Easy Herring Salad

Herring salad is a must on every Christmas morning breakfast table or *julebord*. This one is especially easy because it starts with a jar of marinated herring or herring in wine sauce.

EASY HERRING SALAD

- 1 large jar (about 1 lb.) marinated herring or herring in wine sauce
- 6 pickled beets   .
- 1 sour apple
- 2 dill pickles
- 6 small boiled potatoes
- 1 onion
- ⅓ cup beet juice
- ¼ tsp. pepper

SALAD DRESSING:
- ⅞ cup sour half and half or yoghurt
- 2 tsp. grated horseradish

Makes 10–12 buffet-style servings.

Drain herring and discard onions from the jar.

Cube herring, beets, apple, pickles and potatoes and chop onion. Mix with beet juice and sprinkle with pepper. Place on a dish and garnish with egg.

Mix salad dressing and serve separately.

Easy Herring Platter

This modern recipe is a colorful addition to the Christmas table. It takes only minutes to assemble.

EASY HERRING PLATTER

1 large jar (1 lb.) marinated herring or herring in wine sauce
3 hard-boiled eggs, chopped
2 scallions, chopped
1 small green pepper, chopped
1 small red pepper, chopped
1 cucumber, quartered, seeded and sliced

SAUCE:
¼ cup mayonnaise
¼ cup light cream
1 T. curry powder
8 cocktail onions
Makes 10–12 buffet-style servings.

Arrange drained herring filets in the center of a glass dish. Mix sauce and pour over herring. Mound the vegetables in separate piles around the herring.

Marinated Anchovies

Swedish anchovies are milder than those from Italy or Portugal, so you may want to rinse your anchovies before marinating them.

MARINATED ANCHOVIES

5 tins anchovy filets (2 oz.), drained
Fresh or dried dill for garnish

Blend mustard, vinegar and paprika. Add oil drop by drop, beating constantly to make a mayonnaise-type sauce. Stir in finely chopped onion. Pour over drained anchovy filets.

MARINADE:
¾ *tsp. light Dijon-style mustard*
1½ *tsp. vinegar*
¼ *tsp. paprika*
3 *T. oil, at room temperature*
½ *small red onion, finely chopped*
Makes 14–16 buffet-style servings

Let marinate for at least 2 hours before serving. Garnish with chopped dill.

Elise's Tomatsild☆

Herring in tomato sauce is second only to *sursild*☆ in Norway.

ELISE'S HERRING IN TOMATO SAUCE

6 *filets* kryddersild☆ *or 2 (6 oz.) jars matjes herring (See Notes on Herring, Page 137.)*
1 *onion, sliced*
5–10 *black peppercorns*
1 *bay leaf*
¼ *cup vinegar*
2 *T. water*
½ *cup sugar*
¼ *cup tomato paste*
1 *T. vegetable oil*
Makes 8–10 buffet-style servings.

Cut herring into 1″ pieces and place in a jar with onion, peppercorns and bay leaf. Bring vinegar, water and sugar to a boil. Remove from heat. Stir in tomato paste while still warm. After the tomato mixture has cooled, add oil.
Pour over herring, cover and chill overnight before serving.

Kalvaladåb°

For those who find *sylte*☆ too heavy and too much trouble to prepare, this veal and pork in aspic is a good alternative for the Christmas cold table.

VEAL AND PORK IN ASPIC

2 lbs. lean pork shoulder, preferably with some rind, as this is a good source of gelatin.
2¼ lbs. veal shank or neck, sliced
6 cups of water
3 tsp. salt
1 onion, quartered
1 large carrot
3 cloves
1 bay leaf
6 white peppercorns
6 allspice berries
Serves 10, 16 if buffet-style.

Place pork and veal in a pot just large enough to hold without empty space. Cut meat into pieces, if necessary. Add water to cover, preferably not more than 6 cups. Bring to a boil and skim well. Add salt, onion, carrot and spices. Cover and simmer on low heat for about 1 hour, until meat is tender. Remove meat and let cool. Remove bone, fat and gristle and return meat to broth. Simmer for around 30 minutes to concentrate broth. Remove meat and cut into even cubes. Strain broth, wash out pot and return broth and meat. Simmer for 5 minutes. Pour into a 2½ quart mold and chill. This meat aspic keeps for around 5 days if refrigerated. *Kalvaladåb°* can be frozen, but it must be brought to the boiling point and remolded before serving.

Red Christmas Salad

This is a winter cole slaw for those who would like a colorful salad for the Christmas table without the traditional herring.

RED CHRISTMAS SALAD

3 medium carrots
¼ lb. chunk rutabaga
2–3 beets
½ lb. cabbage
⅓ cup raisins
⅓ cup chopped walnuts

Peel carrots, rutabaga and beets. Coarsely grate carrots, rutabaga, and cabbage. Grate beets separately, as the color runs. Mix together carrots, rutabaga, cabbage, raisins and walnuts.

DRESSING:
3 T. mayonnaise
1½ T. cider vinegar
¼ cup water
1½ tsp. sugar
½ tsp. caraway seeds
Makes 10–12 buffet-style
servings

Mix ingredients for salad dressing and add to vegetable mixture. Fold in beets just before serving.

Rødkålsalat°,

This is a modern salad, but it is a delicious addition to the Christmas cold table. Many Scandinavians include a cold vegetable and fruit salad, such as this one or a waldorf salad, because it is a good accompaniment to cold *ribbe*☆, ham or turkey.

RED CABBAGE SLAW

¾ lb. red cabbage, shredded
2 apples, shredded
1 tsp. caraway seed
1 orange, free of membrane, in sections
¼ cup chopped dates
¼ cup chopped figs (or white raisins)
½ cup sour cream or yogurt
¼ cup mayonnaise
Makes 10–12 buffet-style servings.

Place all ingredients in a large bowl. Mix sour cream and mayonnaise well and pour over ingredients. Chill before serving.

Easy Liver Terrine

The Christmas breakfast table is incomplete without liver paté. Traditionally, this was made with pork liver, but today, chicken liver makes a milder, modern version of this old favorite.

EASY LIVER TERRINE

1 lb. chicken livers
½ cup butter
8 oz. mushrooms
1 medium onion, chopped
¼ cup light cream
¼ cup sherry
Salt and pepper
Pinch nutmeg
2 T. butter

Makes 14–16 buffet-style servings.

Clean, rinse and dry livers. Saute livers in some of the butter and remove from heat while still rosy inside. Saute onions and mushrooms lightly.

Puree livers, mushrooms and onions in a blender or food processor. Add butter gradually, then cream and sherry. Add salt, pepper and nutmeg to taste. Pack in a terrine. Melt butter and pour a thin layer over liver paté. Refrigerate until serving. Do not allow this liver terrine to stand indefinitely at room temperature. This terrine keeps 3–4 days in the refrigerator.

Omens and Predictions

Omens and superstitions were a part of everyday life in Scandinavia 100 years ago, and both were connected with every facet of the Christmas preparations. The most common predictions regarded the most important factors of life: The weather, crops, birth, death and marriage. Many omens and predictions were made on Christmas Day, because the people felt that Christmas was instilled with magic powers which man could harness to an extent, and through these he could read the future. This concept is probably a remnant of the pre-Christian tradition. Omens also were read on New Year's Day, for it was desirable to get a glimpse into the future at the beginning of the new year.

There were two kinds of omens and predictions: those which evaluated natural phenomena, and those in which a situation was constructed for a particular explanation.

The most important of the former concerned the weather. Predictions about the weather have been made since the beginning of history, and these were especially important in Scandinavia because of its heritage of harsh winters and famine. Most of the predictions about the weather involved observations of random signs. Opposites were supposed to hold true: If Christmas were white, then Easter would be green. The saying, "*Julesommer gir påskevinter*☆," "Christmas summer brings Easter winter," dates from the Middle Ages in Norway. If there were a lot of snow at Christmas, the summer would be dry. Other widespread beliefs included: If the branches hung heavily with snow at Christmas or at the New Year, they would hang heavy with fruit in the fall. People in some areas believed that if there were mild weather at Christmas, the grain would rot in the fall, while those in other areas thought just the opposite.

Omens pertaining to life and death sometimes involved a degree of magic, but the Scandinavians never made any study of astrology.

The hearth was the center of the household, and the open fire was a source of light as well as heat. Most of the activities of the home took place around it, and at Christmas it took on mystical powers. Omens were read in the billows of smoke coming from the chimneys: The house with the thickest smoke was thought to get the longest grain next harvest. The first house to finish cooking the Christmas dinner would be the first to harvest its crops next fall. If the smoke took the shape of a cradle, a baby would be born during the coming year; if it looked like a coffin, someone would die. If the fire went out suddenly, death would descend upon the household. It was important for the happiness of the family that the fire burn as clearly and as brightly as possible. Ashes from the Christmas fire were saved and read for predictions: If the pile were large, the harvest next fall would be bountiful. In some areas it was believed that evil spirits entered a house through the chimney, so it was necessary to build as big and as hot a fire as possible to keep them out. There was no room for Santa to come down the chimney in rural Scandinavia in the 18th and 19th centuries.

Omens regarding life and death also were read in candles, for the burning candle was thought to be the flame of life. If the flame burned clear and strong, it was a good sign; if the flame extinguished too soon, it was a sign of impending death. The old tallow candles did not burn evenly, so there was much "food for prediction." In the *grenljus*°, family candles of rural Sweden, one could predict the longevity of the entire family according to how long each branch burned. Sometimes a candle was placed alongside each guest at the Christmas table. The person whose candle burned out first would be the first to die.

Some predictions were fairly easy to manipulate: The more one ate at Christmas, the better year the farm would have. If one held a coin at the stroke of the New Year, he would get happiness and money in the year to come.

Other predictions were more contrived, such as this one from Hallingdal, Norway: Bowls of beer, milk and water were placed on a table. A young girl was blindfolded and told to drink from one of the bowls. If she chose beer, her husband would be a wealthy man; if she chose milk, he would be average; if she chose water, he would be poor. Many predictions involving marriage were made on St. Lucia's day as well.

Christmas Greetings

Since Christmas is a time for renewing family ties, and families no longer live on the same farm or even in the same town as they once did, the Christmas card has become very important to present-day Scandinavians. For many, the annual Christmas card or letter is the only time there is any contact, and writing them is an important preparation for the holiday.

Although the first Christmas card was issued in England as early as 1843, the custom of sending greeting cards did not come to Scandinavia until around 1870, and did not become well established until the turn of the century. Most early cards were from Germany, but by

This Christmas man with his tree, toys, and birch rods resembles our own Santa Claus to a great degree. His hat may be very practical in the frozen north, but it is not what we expect to see, even in Scandinavia.

the early 1880's publishers in Denmark and Sweden had begun to print cards and Norway soon followed. Many of the earlier cards feature snow-covered landscapes and people on skis, winter themes rather than exclusively Christmas topics. By the end of the 19th century, many Scandinavians had emigrated to the U.S. and sent Christmas cards to their families in the "old country." Many of these cards featured decorated Christmas trees and of course, Santa Claus. These, plus the profusion of cards from Germany, many of which featured international Christmas themes such as St. Nicholas and Father Christmas, contributed to the present-day picture of the Scandinavian *nisse**/ *tomte*°.

The early Scandinavian Christmas cards were postcards, and the same is true today. It is the postcard which is the chief form of Christmas greeting throughout Scandinavia. During the month of December, the Post Offices of Norway, Sweden and Denmark have special low rates for postcards containing only these five words: *God jul og godt nyttår**/ *God jul och gott nyttår*°, Merry Christmas and Happy New Year, plus a signature.

St. Stephen's Day

December 26, the second day of Christmas, is called *Stefansdag*☆/ *Staffansdag*○, in honor of the stallboy to Herodes who first saw the star of Bethlehem. St. Stephen was the first Christian martyr and is patron saint of horses. This day, which was dedicated to horses and racing, was celebrated in Scandinavia from the Middle Ages until this century, when the tractor and the automobile replaced horses.

This day marks the transition from the religious celebration to the secular. On St. Stephens day, the holiday entered a livelier phase, starting with St. Stephen's ride, known as *Staffansritt*○ in Sweden. The young men of the farm got up early and raced their horses to a northern running brook, where the water was supposed to be endowed with special powers bestowed by Jesus. The first horse to drink from this water was protected by its magic for the next year.

It was the boys' turn to ride the horses to church and they often had races on the way home. Young men used this day for visiting other farms, offering to clean the barn in exchange for food and drink. Races often were held in the afternoon as well.

Julestuer☆/*julgiller*○, Christmas socials, began on the second day of Christmas. Friends, often everyone who lived in a settlement, gathered together for games, dancing, playing cards and telling stories. These parties moved from house to house and were held sometimes every night until January 6. To *leke*☆/*lege*○ *jul*☆, to "play Christmas" was important, and the games were considered more important than the food and drink, although there was no lack of refreshment at these parties. Sometimes a *julebukk*☆ came to entertain (See *Julebukk*☆. page 124.) and wealthier families sometimes hired small theater groups to entertain or held formal dances. Young people had their own parties.

Julestuer☆ originated in the vigils of the Catholic period, when everyone had to stay awake until Midnight Mass. People passed the time by playing games, drinking, singing and dancing. In the 17th and 18th

Christmas is a time for enjoying the company of family and friends. Note the fiddler sitting on a keg of beer. The young girls who are serving drinks all wear small crowns, rather like Lucia.

centuries laws forbidding these parties on holy days and their eves were passed, so they were postponed until after December 25.

Slottstek med Gräddsås°

Few main dishes are more *helsvensk*°, completely Swedish, than this beef roast with cream sauce, flavored with anchovies. It is a favorite dinner for the second day of Christmas, December 26. Serve with homemade mashed potatoes and lingonberry preserves.

SWEDISH POT ROAST WITH CREAM SAUCE

3 lb. beef roast, preferably eye of round or another long and narrow cut
1 T. vegetable oil
1 large red onion, chopped

Heat oil in a dutch oven. When almost smoking brown meat on all sides very thoroughly. Pound spices in a mortar and add with vegetables and brown lightly. Add 1 cup stock, anchovies, jelly and vi-

1 carrot, scraped and sliced
10 white peppercorns
6 allspice berries
1 bay leaf
1 tin (2 oz.) anchovy filets, drained (Swedish anchovies are milder than those from Italy or Portugal so you may want to rinse these filets before adding).
2 cups beef stock
2 T. red currant jelly
2 T. vinegar
2 T. flour, preferably instant blending
2 cups heavy cream
Salt (omit if anchovies are very salty) and pepper
Serves 6–8.

negar. Cover and braise on low heat, turning several times while cooking. Add more stock as needed.

Allow at least 1½ hours cooking time, but if the roast is compact, rather than long, it may take longer to cook

Remove roast from oven and wrap in foil. Let rest for at least 10 minutes before slicing. Strain pan juices—they ought to measure about 1¼ cups. Boil down if there is more.

Slottstek° can be prepared in advance up to this point. To serve, slice meat thinly and heat gently in beef stock.

To make gravy, add flour to pan juices, bring to a boil and add cream. Cook for 6–8 minutes, stirring constantly. Do not allow to boil over. Add salt and pepper to taste.

Rutabaga Pudding

This is a Finnish variation of mashed rutabagas, which is delicious with roast meat. The sugar offsets the slightly bitter taste of the rutabaga.

RUTABAGA PUDDING

2 rutabagas (about 1½ lbs each)
¼ cup dry breadcrumbs
¼ cup evaporated milk or half and half
¼ tsp. nutmeg
1 tsp. salt
1½ tsp. sugar
2 eggs, beaten
2–3 T. butter
Serves 8.

Peel and dice rutabagas. There should be about 6 cups. Cook covered in a small amount of lightly salted water until soft, about 15–20 minutes. Drain and mash. Preheat oven to 350°F.

Mix remaining ingredients with mashed rutabaga and mix well.

Pour into a buttered 2½ quart casserole, dot with butter and bake for approximately 1 hour, or until puffed and lightly browned.

Poached Cod

Not everyone has access to fresh cod, but frozen cod can be prepared in a similar way. Prepare frozen steaks (on the bone) just as you would fresh cod, but allow 1–2 minutes additional cooking time. Add 1 T. vinegar to the water to firm the flesh. With both fresh and frozen fish, timing is very important. Do not overcook, or you will end up with scrambled, tasteless flakes. Serve cod with boiled potatoes, melted parsley butter and marinated cucumber salad. This is a lovely light meal after all the heavy pork dishes.

POACHED COD

1 (1 lb.) block frozen boneless cod (at least partially thawed), sliced into serving portions
1 T. salt
1 T. vinegar
Serves 3.

Pour water into a skillet to a depth of ½". Add salt and vinegar and bring to a boil. Place cod in the water and remove immediately from the heat. Let sit for 6–8 minutes or until just done.

Ris á la Malta*

Cold rice porridge and whipped cream pair to make an easy and delicious holiday dessert. Scandinavians usually serve this with a sauce made from thickened fruit syrups. Berry purees make a tasty substitute.

RICE Á LA MALTA

4 cups cold rice porridge
2 cups whipping cream
1 tsp. vanilla

Whip cream and blend with porridge. Add vanilla and sugar. Serve in individual glass bowls.

FRUIT SAUCE FOR RICE Á LA MALTA

2 packages (10 oz.) frozen raspberries or strawberries (thawed) or 1 of each
3 T. sugar
3 T. cornstarch
¼ cup water

Puree berries. Add sugar and heat to boiling. Combine cornstarch and water and stir into berries. Cook until thickened, stirring constantly. Cool and pour into a pitcher to serve.

The New Year

It is only in the 20th century that the New Year is regarded as a completely separate secular holiday. In the Christian calendar and in the old Nordic calendar sticks, *primstaver*☆/*runstavar*○, the year began at Christmas, and January 1 was long considered the eighth day of Christmas.

While Christmas was a family feast, the New Year was a time to celebrate with friends, and New Year's Eve is still the favorite night of the year for parties. Many Christmas traditions hold true for the New Year as well in Scandinavia. Gifts were sometimes exchanged, for the practice of gift-giving as we know it originated with the Roman New Year. Omens were "read," and many stayed awake all night, not to welcome the birth of the Christ child, but to make sure that the Day of Judgment did not arrive.

Two small boys light a firecracker to "shoot in the New Year."

In some areas the New Year, *nyttår*✧/*nyår*°, was considered a more auspicious time than Christmas for predicting the future. In many parts of Sweden, people ate an apple on New Year's morning to keep healthy for the rest of the year. Maybe they knew about the old saying, "An apple a day keeps the doctor away," but in Sweden a century ago apples were a winter luxury, and one apple would have to do until harvest time in the fall. If the weather were good on New Year's Day, it would continue to be good for the rest of the year. The same reasoning was used for people. However one felt on New Year's Day would be decisive for the rest of the year.

The shooting of a New Year's salute was first practiced by the military for the King of Denmark and Sweden on New Year's morning. People sometimes shot in the New Year privately either on the morning of January 1 or at 5 p.m. on New Year's Eve. Displays of fireworks have replaced this custom, and they are a colorful part of the New Year celebration in most cities and towns throughout Scandinavia.

New Year's Day is a formal visiting time, and citizens who want to pay their respect to the King and Queen of Sweden can sign the guest book at the royal palace in Stockholm. The royal families of all three Scandinavian countries appear on television to wish a Happy New Year to their subjects.

Until around 1915, New Year's cards were more popular than Christmas cards in Scandinavia. This was probably because Christmas was more of a family occasion, and greetings to friends came later in the celebration of the holiday season. Good luck symbols of all kinds appear on these old cards, some familiar, some more unusual. Bears are featured on many, for according to legend the bear rolls over in his den on New Year's Day, marking the middle of winter. Chimney sweeps and mushrooms, traditional European good luck symbols, appear on them as well, along with four-leaf clovers, horseshoes, apples, coins and champagne.

Stekt Rype✧

Many Scandinavians, Norwegians in particular, like to have roast ptarmigan for one dinner during the Christmas season. If ptarmigan are unavailable, try preparing cornish hens in this manner for a change of pace. Appropriate side dishes are boiled potatoes, brussels sprouts, lingonberry preserves or currant jelly and a full-bodied red wine.

PTARMIGAN

2 ptarmigan or cornish hens

1 tsp. salt

2 thin pieces barding fat (cornish hens—2 strips of bacon)

Butter or margarine for browning

SAUCE:

⅔ cup boiling water

1 cup milk

¾ cup sour cream

1½ T. all-purpose flour

1½ T. butter

Several slices geitost☆, brown goat cheese

Cooked livers from the birds

1 T. red currant jelly

Gizzards and hearts from the birds

Serves 4.

Clean birds. Scandinavian birds are usually sold feathered. Rather than plucking them, the Scandinavian housewife usually skins them, thus the importance of barding fat for these lean game birds. Wash and dry, inside and out. Bind barding fat or bacon over breasts.

Heat butter in a heavy skillet and brown birds well. Add gizzards, hearts, water and milk. Turn birds breast up, cover and simmer until tender, about 1 hour. Toward the end of the cooking time, add sour cream and geitost☆. Remove birds when done and keep warm.

Make beurre manie with the flour and butter and whisk into cooking liquid. Saute liver, mash and add to cooking liquid with jelly. Finely chop gizzards and hearts and add to the sauce.

Pigs' Trotters

Most Scandinavians buy half a pig every autumn, so they automatically have two trotters for "nattmat☆," night food, for New Year's Eve or for the Christmas table. These are a bit of trouble to make, so you may prefer to buy them readymade.

Trotters are usually served cold with mustard and pickled vegetables, with lomper☆ or flatbread on the side. They also can be breaded and baked. Trotters are finger food at its very best. They are always served with beer.

You may have to order trotters from your butcher.

PIGS' TROTTERS

2 trotters

BRINE:
1 quart water
6–7 T. sugar
⅓ cup sugar
3 bay leaves
Serves 4.

Wash, scrape and remove any bristles from the trotters. Soak in cold water for around 6 hours. Simmer in plain water for about 2 hours. Cool quickly by placing in cold water.

Make brine and soak trotters in it for at least 3 days before serving. To serve, divide lengthwise.

Multekrem☆/Hjortrongrädde○

Cloudberries in cream is a classic of the Scandinavian kitchen, which tastes spectacular any time of year. These orange berries, which grow in the swamplands of Norway, Sweden and Finland, have a taste unlike any other. For an extra touch to this simple but elegant dish, add a dash of *lakka,* cloudberry liqueur from Finland or Sweden.

CLOUDBERRIES IN CREAM

2 cups fresh or canned cloudberries or cloudberry jam
2 cups whipping cream
Sugar to taste
3 T. cloudberry liqueur (optional)
Serves 6.

Whip cream and blend in berries. Add sugar to taste. Stir in liqueur. Serve in individual glass bowls. Garnish with a few whole berries.

Note: This dessert can be made with lingonberries as well. Then it is called *trollkrem*☆, cream of the trolls.

Starboys

January 6, the Feast of the Epiphany, also called the Feast of the Three Kings, was traditionally a visiting day. The early Christians celebrated this day as Christ's birthday. Three-armed candles, *helligtrekongerslys*☆/-*ljus*○, were lit for this occasion in honor of the three kings who visited the Christ child, the light of the world. This day also marks the celebration of Christ's baptism. Today three-armed candlesticks, which are easier to obtain than the special branch candles, decorate many tables.

This was the most important day for performances of the *stjernegutter*☆/*stjärngosser*○/*stjernedrenge*◇, as the three kings were the central figures of their pageant. The starboys originated in Germany and France in the Middle Ages, and their pageant evolved from the mystery and miracle plays of the time. Because it was easier to convey the story of Christmas in actions than in words, the drama was taken out of the church and given to the people. These boys dressed up as the three kings plus Mary, Joseph, St. Stephen, Herodes and others, and sang songs and gave dialogues. The leader held a pole topped with a large star, which was lit before each house the boys visited, thus their name, starboys. Because of the importance of the star, they sometimes performed on St. Stephen's day and continued their pageants until January 6. By necessity this was an urban tradition and was therefore more popular in Denmark and Sweden than in Norway. Eventually the schools took over the tradition from the churches in Protestant countries. These boys performed throughout the year at weddings and other festive occasions, and in Denmark they had a royal dispensation allowing them to earn money in this way. Because everyone was generous at Christmas, they usually collected for their services of the previous year at that time. After the middle of the 18th century, the boys no longer were paid to appear, and their performances became less religious. This custom died out in Denmark, but in Sweden the star boys have become part of the Lucia procession.

Today, boys' choirs, sometimes called *stjernegutter**, give concerts in churches at Christmas throughout Scandinavia.

Lutefisk* Soufflé

Make a light soufflé from leftover *lutefisk**. The fish must be well-drained—it can even be slightly dried out before adding to the souffle mixture.

LUTEFISK SOUFFLÉ

2 cups lutefisk, without skin and bones and well-drained*
2 T. butter
2 T. all-purpose flour
1¼ cups half and half
1 tsp. salt
⅛ tsp. pepper
pinch allspice
4 egg yolks
6 egg whites
1 T. cornstarch

For a 2 quart straight-sided soufflé dish:
1 T. butter
1 T. flour
Serves 6.

Melt 2 T. butter in a stainless steel or enamel saucepan. (Aluminum will discolor mixture.) Add flour and cook for 1 minute, but do not allow to brown. Add half and half gradually, whisking well until thickened. Boil for 2 minutes. Do not allow to boil over. Remove from heat and add egg yolks, one at a time, then salt, pepper and allspice. Stir occasionally until the mixture is cool.

Preheat oven to 400°F.

Carefully add the cleaned *lutefisk** to the egg yolk mixture, stirring as little as possible.

Stiffly beat egg whites and fold in cornstarch. Fold ⅓ of whites into egg yolk mixture, then fold in the rest. Pour the mixture into a well-greased and floured soufflé dish. Spread evenly with a spatula. Place on bottom rack and bake for 35 minutes. Serve with melted butter.

Stephen was a Stallboy drawn by A. Malmström. A procession of starboys in Sweden. The stylized border features drinking horns, gingerbread figures and a *tomte*° woven into the revived viking style ornament.

Glaserat Revbensspjäll°

The Swedes love ribs, too. Their spareribs are more like the American variety, without the bacon attached. Traditionally they are served with plumped prunes and kale.

GLAZED SPARERIBS

4 lbs. spareribs
2 tsp. salt
½ tsp. black pepper

GLAZE:
½ cup black or red currant jelly (grape can be substituted)
2 T. Dijon-style mustard
2 T. regular prepared mustard
Serves 6–8.

Preheat oven to 450°F.
Salt and pepper ribs and place in roasting pan. Roast for about 1 hour. Drain off fat. Melt jelly, add mustards and mix. Brush glaze over ribs and continue baking for 10 minutes. The sugar content of the jelly makes it burn easily, so watch closely.

Brunkål°

This is a delicious, lower calorie version of brown cabbage, which is made in the oven. This dish freezes well.

BROWNED CABBAGE

1 head cabbage (about 4 lbs.)
2 onions
2 T. oil or other fat
4 T. vinegar
2 T. soy sauce
2 T. corn syrup
2 tsp. ground allspice
Stock or bouillon
Serves 16.

Preheat oven to 425°F.
Shred cabbage and cook for about 10 minutes in lightly salted water. Drain well. Coat the bottom of a deep pan, such as a broiler or roaster, with oil. Spread cabbage evenly in pan. Sprinkle with vinegar and soy sauce and drizzle with syrup. Sprinkle with allspice.
Bake for around 2 hours, until the cabbage is evenly colored. Mix well several times during cooking. Cabbage may need extra stock if it begins to dry out, or for reheating.

Sultana Cake

This fruited pound cake is a lighter Scandinavian alternative to our fruitcake.

SULTANA CAKE

1 cup margarine
1 cup sugar
3 eggs
⅔ cup raisins dusted with
  2 T. flour
⅓ cup blanched and sliv-
  ered almonds
⅓ cup candied orange
  peel, chopped
⅓ cup candied citron,
  chopped
1½ cups all-purpose flour
½ tsp. baking powder
Serves 12.

Preheat oven to 350°F.

Cream margarine and sugar well. Add eggs, one at a time, and beat well after each. Add fruit and nuts, then flour and baking powder. Pour into a greased and floured small tube pan. Bake 35–40 minutes. Let cool for 10 minutes before removing from pan.

Julebukk

Sometimes the starboys were accompanied by a *julebukk*☆/*julbock*◇/ *julebuk*◇, a person dressed in a pelt wearing a large goat's head mask complete with horns and beard, who acted as a kind of buffoon and made a spectacle. This character resembled the devilish figure, Krampus, who sometimes accompanied St. Nicholas on his rounds in central Europe—in some areas of Scandinavia it was a person dressed as a *julebukk*☆ who distributed presents, but he was overshadowed by the gift-bringing *julenisse*☆/*jultomte*◇.

The *julebukk*☆ mask is a remnant from pagan times, when animal masks were associated with infernal powers. The attributes of the devil were transferred to the *julebukk*☆, and it is in this context that he appears in the pageant of the starboys. He is the foil to these figures who symbolize victory of Christ over the powers of evil.

In rural Norway, a person dressed as a *julebukk*☆ often visited the farms to entertain and to demand food and drink. This travelling comedian/troubadour was a welcome guest and an important part of the *julestuer*☆, which were held in the period between Christmas and the New Year. Sometimes he enjoyed himself so much that he took off his costume and joined in the merrymaking.

Today children play *julebukk*☆ by dressing in costume and going from house to house demanding cookies, much as American children go trick-or-treating on Halloween. Now they dress up just to hide their

Christmas in Sweden by A. Malmström and G. Broling. From the top: A tiny *tomte*◇ sits in the loft enjoying his Christmas porridge. A *julbokk*◇ distributes presents, while a woman prepares the piles of bread for the Christmas table. Note the three-armed candle. The Christmas tree is exceptionally large, considering the date, 1867. It is unlikely that many rural homes had trees at that time. The artists were probably from Stockholm and incorporated this almost exclusively urban tradition into their drawing of a country Christmas. Church services often began before dawn, and people rode on their sleighs by torchlight. Legend says that the bear turns over in his sleep at the New Year, thus the bear in the lower left. The dog on the right is just to balance the bear and has no particular significance at Christmas. The bottom vignettes illustrated the Christmas rush in the city and the visit of the starboys. One boy is opening his purse to collect coins from the crowd.

identity, not to look scary. Parties of other kinds—*julgransplyndringer*°, harvesting the Christmas tree in Sweden, and *pepperkakehusfester*☆, dismantling and eating the gingerbread house, have all but replaced the wanderings of small *julebukker*☆ in most urban areas. But the object is the same—to eat the last of the Christmas food.

Serve these delicate cookies in your own *julestue*☆:

Drömmer°

"Dreams" are a Swedish cookie with a special flavor from browned butter. These drop cookies are easy to make.

"DREAMS"

1 cup cold butter
1¼ cups sugar
½ tsp. vanilla
¼ tsp. hornsalt (See Notes on Baking, Page 137.)
2⅓ cups all-purpose flour
Makes about 40 cookies.

Brown butter in a skillet—do not allow to burn. Cool until hardened. Preheat oven to 300°F.
Cream butter and sugar and add vanilla. Add hornsalt and flour to make a dough. Form small mounds with 2 spoons. Place on ungreased cookie sheet. Bake 25–30 minutes. Store in an airtight tin.

Kokosmakroner☆

Coconut macaroons are international, and what better way can you find to use up the egg whites from the *berlinerkranser*☆? (Page 56.)

COCONUT MACAROONS

4 egg whites
1 cup sugar
2½ cups coconut
Makes around 40 cookies.

Preheat oven to 350°F.
Beat egg whites until stiff. Add sugar gradually, and beat into a thick, stiff meringue. Stir in coconut and pour into a saucepan. Stir over medium heat until mixture thickens.
Place spoonfuls of the mixture on a greased and floured cookie sheet. Bake for 10–12 minutes.

Sandkaker*

These tart shells are made in fluted forms that can be purchased in specialty stores. They are traditionally served stacked upside down. They also can be filled with berries and whipped cream for a delicious dessert.

These *sandkaker** are made with egg, but without nuts.

SANDKAKER

1 cup soft butter
1 cup sugar
1 egg
1 tsp. almond extract (optional)
2½ cups all-purpose flour
Makes about 40 *sandkaker**.

Cream butter and sugar until light and fluffy. Add egg and almond extract. Add flour to make a stiff dough. Chill for at least 1 hour.
Preheat oven to 350°F.
Press dough into greased *sandkake** forms with a floured finger. Place forms on a cookie sheet. Bake for 12–15 minutes or until just golden. Cool slightly before removing from forms. Store in an airtight tin.

Sandkaker*

These *sandkaker** are made with both egg and nuts.

SANDKAKER

¾ cup butter
½ cup sugar
1 egg yolk
½ cup ground almonds
1⅔ cups all-purpose flour
Makes about 35 cookies.

Cream butter and sugar until light and fluffy. Add egg yolk and beat well. Add nuts and flour, and mix thoroughly. Chill for at least 1 hr.
Preheat oven to 350°F
Press dough into greased *sandkake** forms with a floured finger. Bake for 12–15 minutes, or until just golden. Cool slightly before removing from forms. Store in an airtight tin.

Finska Pinnar°

These Finnish cookies are popular in Sweden as well. Butter cookies are always delicious, and these are encrusted with chopped almonds and pearl sugar.

FINNISH STICKS

1 cup soft butter
½ cup sugar
1 egg
1 tsp. almond extract
Pinch salt
3 cups all-purpose flour
Beaten egg or egg white
Pearl sugar or crushed
  sugar cubes
1½ cups finely chopped
  almonds

Makes about 60 cookies.

Preheat oven to 350°F.
Cream butter and sugar until light and fluffy. Add egg, almond extract and salt. Add flour and mix well to distribute the butter throughout the dough.
Shape into long, finger-thick rolls. Cut into 3" lengths. Dip in beaten egg, then sugar, then almonds. Place on a greased cookie sheet. Bake for 8–10 minutes or until just beginning to brown. Store in an airtight tin.

Hjortetakk☆

These small doughnuts are named for the leavening agent used to bake them, *hjortetakksalt*☆ or hornsalt (See Notes on Baking, page 137.) These cookies can be frozen for a short time and taste newly baked if warmed up in the oven before serving.

HORNSALT RINGS

1 egg plus 1 egg yolk
½ cup sugar
¼ cup whipping cream
3 T. butter
¼ tsp. cardamon
¼ tsp. hornsalt
2½ cups all-purpose flour
Oil or fat for frying

Makes 45–50 cakes.

Beat egg with sugar. Whip cream and melt butter. Mix together. Add cardamon and stir in flour and hornsalt, blending well. Sprinkle with flour and chill overnight. Roll into 4–5" lengths about ½" thick. Make small doughnuts. Cut several nicks along the outside edge. Heat oil or fat to 350°F. Fry until golden brown on both sides. Drain on paper towels.

Christmas in Norway by Vilhelm Peters, 1887. These vignettes are framed in the woodcarving style of the viking ships and stave churches, which was revived in the middle of the 19th century. From the top: The placement of the Julenek marks the beginning of Christmas. The sleigh is being prepared for a visit to a neighbouring farm. In the center the starboys and the julebukk pay a visit. The children are afraid of the masked figures—the little girl covers her face, and the boy runs away from them.

St. Knud's Day

St. Knud was a Danish duke who was killed in battle on January 7, 1131 and was canonized 38 years later. He is remembered chiefly because the 13th day of Christmas falls on his day. Old almanacs show that Knud's day was moved from January 7 to January 13 at the end of the 17th century, and in some places this day is considered to be the last day of the holiday.

All Christmas food and beer was supposed to last until Knud's day. The family circled the Christmas tree for the last time before it was stripped of the last edible decorations and thrown out. The women of the house took down the Christmas wall decorations, opened all the doors and windows, and literally swept the last remains of Christmas out of the house.

In Småland, Sweden, all bones from the Christmas meat were cooked to make a soup, which was served with *doppebröd*°, bread for dipping, on the Sunday nearest St. Knud's day.

Until the middle of the 19th century, people in Norway and western Sweden dedicated a *skål*☆ to Eldbjørk—not to a person, as it sounds, but to the spirit of the fire. Husband and wife drank first and then cast a spoonful of the last of the Christmas beer onto the fire. Fire is *ild*☆ in Scandinavian, and *bjørk*☆ is birch, so the origin of the word is understandable.

There is no real tradition associated with this day, but it is a good time to hold a *julgransplyndring*° or a *pepperkakehusfest*☆ where children are invited to strip the Christmas tree or to dismantle and eat the gingerbread house.

Köttbullar°

No *smörgåsbord*° is complete without Swedish meatballs and all children love them. This basic recipe can be used with your choice of

Farewell to the Christmas Tree by A. E., 1891. The children take one last look at the once festive Christmas tree, now ready to be carted away. Alongside the tree is a broom for "sweeping out" the last remnants of the holiday.

gravy. They make a delicious dinner served with boiled potatoes, pickles, pickled beets and lingonberry preserves. These meatballs freeze well.

SWEDISH MEATBALLS

1 lb. meatloaf mixture (½ beef, ½ pork)
⅓ cup breadcrumbs
⅓ cup water or milk
1 large cooked potato
1 onion
1 egg
1 tsp. salt
⅛ tsp. white pepper
⅛ tsp. sugar
Margarine for frying
Serves 4, 8 if buffet-style.

Soak crumbs in water or milk. Finely grate onion and potato. Mix all ingredients. Make meatballs with 1 T. mixture and place on a greased dish.

Melt margarine in a frying pan over medium-high heat. To keep meatballs round, let them roll from the dish into the hot pan. Shake pan while frying, so that the meatballs never get a chance to "sit." Fry for around 5 minutes.

Sirupssnipper☆

These ginger cookies can be made with used fat. Have these on hand for all the small *julebukker*☆ who come to your end of Christmas party to stretch the remains of the gingerbread house.

GINGER DIAMONDS

½ cup light molasses
½ cup sugar
¼ cup milk
¼ tsp. ginger
¼ tsp. pepper
½ cup butter or fat left from cooking Fattigmann☆ or Hjortetakk☆
3 cups all-purpose flour
½ tsp. baking powder
2 oz. blanched almond halves
Makes around 100 cookies.

Blend molasses, sugar, milk and spices. Melt fat and add. Stir in flour and baking powder, mixing well. Refrigerate several hours or overnight.
Preheat oven to 350°F.
Roll out dough in small amounts, keeping the rest chilled. Use as little flour as possible in rolling out. Make diamond-shaped cookies with a pastry wheel. Place on a greased cookie sheet. Decorate with an almond half in the center.
Bake about 10 minutes, until light brown. Lay flat on a rack to cool. Store in an airtight tin.

Skillingsboller*

This sweet cardamon dough can be used as the basis for a variety of sweet breads and coffee cakes. *Boller**, sweet buns, with and without raisins, are a must at all children's parties in Scandinavia, and *skillingsboller**, which are smaller versions of the above buns, are the usual fare at Christmas tree parties.

SMALL SWEET BUNS

¼ cup butter
2½ cups milk, scalded
2 packages active dry yeast
6½ cups all-purpose flour
2 eggs, beaten
¾ cup sugar
1 tsp. salt
1 tsp. ground cardamon,

GLAZE:
¼ cup confectioner's sugar
¼ cup half and half or milk

Makes 50.

Melt butter in scalded milk. Cool to luke-warm and stir in the yeast. Add 2½ cups flour and beat with a mixer until smooth. Let mixture rest for 30 minutes.

Beat in eggs, sugar, salt and cardamon. Add around 4 cups flour to make a dough. Knead until smooth and elastic, about 10 minutes. Let rise until double, about one hour.

Make 50 balls and place on greased cookie sheets. Let rise until almost triple. Preheat oven to 350°F.

Bake 10–12 minutes. Mix glaze and pour over *skillingsboller** while still warm.

Non-alcoholic Gløgg*

Children and non-drinkers will love this version of *gløgg**.

MULLED JUICES

2 cups black currant juice (available at health food stores) or cranberry juice
2 cups apple juice
5 cloves
1 piece stick cinnamon
⅓ cup raisins
20 blanched almonds
sugar, if necessary

Makes 1 quart.

Warm juices with sugar and spices. Serve with raisins and almonds. This tastes better if the spices can steep in the juices before heating.

Lammerull*

The delicate flavoring of this lamb and sausage roll makes it a year-round favorite for the cold table. Sweep out Christmas with this lovely cold sausage roll.

LAMB AND SAUSAGE ROLL

2 lbs. lamb flank/breast, bones removed and meat cut into an even rectangle.
1½ tsp. salt
½ lb. ground pork sausage
1 egg
1 small can sliced mushrooms in butter
¼ tsp. marjoram
¼ tsp. ginger (omit if sausage is very spicy)
¼ tsp. sage
2 cloves garlic, chopped
2 shallots, chopped

FOR COOKING:
2 to 2½ quarts water
2 T. salt
5 peppercorns
1 onion, in chunks
1 carrot, sliced
2 stalks celery, in 2" lengths
Serves 10.

Pound meat lightly and rub with salt. Lay on flat surface with meaty side up.

Mix sausage with remaining ingredients and spread on meat. Roll loosely, so the sausage is not forced out. Wrap with cheesecloth and tie with string, securing both ends.

Bring water to a boil, add lamb roll and bring again to a boil. Skim, then add salt, pepper and vegetables. Cover and simmer for around 2 hours.

Remove from water and set under a press for at least 12 hours. (If you do not have a press, weigh it down with a dish and some heavy cans.) Slice thinly to serve. This lamb and sausage roll can be frozen for up to one month.

No one shall carry out Christmas drawn by A. Malmström. No traveller was to be denied hospitality at Christmas. Even the animals on the farm should enjoy the bounty of the holiday. Note the many rings of flatbread hanging from the ceiling.

APPENDIX

NOTES ON BAKING

Some of the ingredients in the recipes of this book may be unfamiliar. These definitions should help:

Hornsalt, *hjortetakk*☆, is a leavening agent used in many traditional Norwegian recipes. Chemically, it is ammonium carbonate, and was made originally from antlers. It gives off the odor of ammonia while baking, but there is no trace of it in the finished product. It produces crispy cookies and crackers. It is very volatile and loses its effectiveness quickly. Count on a shelf life of about six months. 3 tsp. baking powder can be substituted for 1 tsp. hornsalt.

Pearl sugar, *pärl sukker*○, are large sugar crystals which are used to decorate cakes and cookies. Crushed sugar cubes can be substituted, but real pearl sugar is more delicate for fancy cookies.

Potato starch is a thickening agent which resembles cornstarch in consistency. It also is used in some cakes and cookies. When cornstarch is substituted for potato starch, it is used in a slightly greater volume, for potato starch is denser. Most of the old recipes were weighed, and it is the weight that has determined the volumetric measurements in this book.

Scandinavian flour is different from American flour. Regular white flour resembles the American unbleached flour, because around 75% of the whole grain is used to make it. In the U.S. only about 55% of the whole grain is used in cake flour, thus it is not suitable for these recipes. Barley flour can be purchased at healthfood stores. It is also a good idea to buy rye flour there, because the coarse grind resembles more closely the Scandinavian rye flour than the usual supermarket variety.

NOTES ON HERRING

Salt herring, *spekesild*☆/*saltsill*○ was once a part of everyone's diet in Scandinavia and even in parts of the U.S. It was cheap and it needed no refrigeration. My mother remembers from childhood the barrels of salt herring at the grocery store. Her mother soaked and fileted the fish and served them with boiled potatoes, pickled beets and sour cream. This is one of those old, everyday dishes which has become a delicacy, because it is just too time consuming to prepare now that the majority of women work.

In Scandinavia, home of the herring, frozen, pre-soaked filets are available, so that everyone can enjoy herring without all the work. These have not yet come to the U.S., and until they do, we will have to use salt herring from the fish market or delicatessen. But there are a few tips and shortcuts that are good to know.

Most of the herring recipes in this book call for old-fashioned salt herring. All salt herring must be soaked in cold water before using. Soaking time varies according to taste, but 12–15 hours ought to be about right. Be sure to change water once or twice. Herring should be soaked whole, for filets tend to disintegrate. Cut off the head and slit the belly to remove the insides before soaking. Place a dish in the bottom of the bowl to raise the fish above the salt, which sinks to the bottom.

Herring is an easy fish to filet. Place the point of a sharp knife against the backbone of the fish at the neck end. With one motion, draw the knife along the backbone to the tail, pressing against the bone at all times, so that little fish is left on it. Turn and repeat on other side. You now have two filets. Remove the small side bones by sliding the knife under the edges of the bones and scraping toward the thin end. Grasp the edge of the skin between the knife and your thumb and peel from neck to tail. It should come off in one piece. Repeat with the other filet. Now the herring filets are ready to use.

Matjes herring is packed in jars fileted and sliced, and can be found in most supermarkets in the U.S. These herring take on a reddish color from the brine and are similar to the Scandinavian *kryddersild*☆ They do not resemble Scandinavian *matjessild*☆ in spite of the name. They are not quite so heavily salted as salt herring, so they need less soaking time, about 8 hours. They are more perishable than salt herring and must be refrigerated.

If you are unable to get either salt herring or matjes herring or don't have the time to pre-soak them. you can still try the herring recipes. Just buy marinated herring or herring in wine sauce, pour off the marinade, discard the onions and rinse the pieces of herring in cold water. Then proceed with the recipe. The taste won't be exactly the same, but it still will be delicious, providing the herring has enough time to absorb the flavor of the new marinade.

BIBLIOGRAPHY

These three books have been an invaluable help to me in researching this book. If you can read any of the Scandinavian languages, I suggest you obtain these for a deeper insight into the Christmas customs of Norway, Denmark and Sweden, respectively.

*Bø, Olav, *Vår norske jul,* Det Norske Samlaget, Oslo, 1974.

◇Pio, Iørn, *Julens hvem hvad hvor,* Politikens Forlag, Copenhagen, 1977.

○Schön, Ebbe, *Julen förr i tiden,* Ljungföretagen, Örebro, 1980.

RECIPE INDEX

Sources of Illustrations

All pictures except for Ills. 5, 15, and where otherwise noted, courtesy Universitets Bibliotek, Oslo